IMAGES
of America

WYOMING COUNTY

Many of the photographs in this book are from the Robert R. Keller collection. Robert (1893–1967) moved to Wyoming County in 1899. From 1910 to 1914, he operated a photography studio in Pineville. In 1914, he married Nellie Ruth Hoover, and they moved to Hinton in Summers County, West Virginia. There he worked for a utilities company, served as a reporter and photographer for an area newspaper, and established an accounting office. He remained an avid photographer into his mid-60s. Many of his images reflect his keen eye for humor, balance, and beauty. (Photograph from the Robert R. Keller collection.)

IMAGES
of America

WYOMING COUNTY

Ed Robinson
Foreword by David "Bugs" Stover, Circuit Court Clerk

ARCADIA
PUBLISHING

Published by Arcadia Publishing
Charleston, South Carolina

Library of Congress Catalog Card Number: 2005926325

For all general information contact Arcadia Publishing at:
Telephone 843-853-2070
Fax 843-853-0044
E-mail sales@arcadiapublishing.com
For customer service and orders:
Toll-Free 1-888-313-2665

Visit us on the Internet at www.arcadiapublishing.com

ACKNOWLEDGMENTS

I am very grateful to the many people who helped me with this book. Foremost I appreciate the help, assistance, advice, and love of my wife, Susan. Also the interest and encouragement of my mother, Frances, was helpful.

I am indebted to three Summers County residents who helped me start the project: Steve Trail, county historian; Barbara Keller, daughter of photographer Robert R. Keller; and Jim Phillips, Pipestem State Park naturalist. Phillips provided introductions to two valuable Wyoming County contacts: Scott Durham, Twin Falls State Park superintendent; and David "Bugs" Stover, circuit court clerk. Stover kindly wrote the foreword to this book and introduced me to Mike Goode, who had a valuable photograph collection.

Wyoming County authors including Paul Blankenship, Epp Cline, Jack Feller, Karl Lilly III, and Bud Perry were most helpful and generous.

Several organizations provided valuable support, including the West Virginia State Archives staff, the R. D. Bailey Lake staff, the Eastern Regional Coal Archives staff, and the officers and members of the Wyoming County Genealogy Society.

I would like also to thank Lauren Bobier, my editor at Arcadia; Kellan Sarles; and Marsha Hannah Thompson for their invaluable assistance.

Other individuals who contributed many photographs to this book include the following: Christy Bailey; Chris Chambers; Lewis D'Antoni; Betty Wylie Farmer; Dorothy Miller Green; Roger Lester; Jean Walker Lusk; Don Nuckols; Marie McKinney Pedneau; Shirley Blankenship Phillips; and Linda Morgan Toler. In addition, I appreciate others, not mentioned previously, who were kind in contributing photographs for the book. In the body of the book, they are credited with their contributions.

Finally, I would like to thank the residents of Wyoming County, whose generosity, courage, and love of history made the project a rewarding experience to the author.

On the Cover: Kopperston miners are pictured relaxing while waiting for the man trip to take them inside the mine. (Photograph courtesy of the National Archives, College Park, Maryland; Still Pictures RG-245-MS-1788L.)

CONTENTS

FOREWORD

Two hundred and forty decades ago, Herodotus wrote a history of the known world. He traveled to the far corners of his world interviewing the common and the great, observing the wonderful and the mundane, and then spent years organizing, writing, and finally publishing the first serious attempt at objective history. When commenting about the reason for such an effort, he wrote, "in the hope of thereby preserving from decay the remembrance of what men have done."

Wyoming County is a land of steep, V-shaped hollows. It has been said that "these hollers are so narrow that a dog has to wag its tail up and down as there ain't room to do it sideways." Flat land exists on ridge tops and an occasional wide bottom along the Guyandotte and its tributaries, usually where streams come together. Along the Clear Fork watershed, though, there are thousands of acres of rich bottomland surrounded by steep mountain forest. Tens of thousands of years ago, this area was a lake, and thousands of years of alluvium from fast moving creeks created, after the lake drained, some of the thickest topsoil in North America.

For thousands of years, people have lived in present-day Wyoming County. A very large town grew up on the lake bed, probably holding sway over much of what was to become the hill country of southern West Virginia, eastern Kentucky, and southwest Virginia. This story is just now coming to light. Many archaeologists believe Native Americans carved petroglyphs (rock drawings) here many centuries before Columbus sailed from Spain. Others believe Celtic people or people who came into contact with the Celts carved the petroglyphs. Eventually Europeans, Americans by then, came scouting through; some finally stayed to farm. By the time whites and some African Americans arrived to stay, Native Americans had mostly departed for the Ohio and Kentucky areas. Timber became king, at first being rafted down the Guyandotte to be sold along the Ohio. Edgar Allen Poe's friend and sometimes enemy Thomas Dunn English wrote an epic poem about the thrill and danger of splash damming logs down the mighty Guyan. Eventually men like William Ritter brought sawmills to places like Maben, and the era of the splash dams was over. Timbering stayed but coal became king, and an epic struggle began for control of the land.

Towns were built because of coal and the railroads that moved it. The story of Wyoming County became the story of Oceana, Pineville, and Mullens, but also of Coal Mountain, and Basin, Glen Rogers, and Herndon, of Sun Hill, Road Branch, Baileysville, Huff Creek, and Pierpoint. The story of Wyoming is the story of the Cooks, Shrewsburys, Lamberts, Goodes, Tolers, Shannons, Stewarts, McGradys, Houcks, Baileys, Woods, McKinneys, and Mullins, and the many thousands who have struggled, failed, and succeeded here.

Ed Robinson has traveled through Wyoming County collecting old pictures and old stories. He is a brilliant and caring man, perfectly suited to his task of "preserving from decay the remembrance of what men, and women, have done." His work, this book, is a valuable addition to the works about this land, Wyoming County, we call home.

—David "Bugs" Stover

INTRODUCTION

Many people regard Wyoming County as the hidden gem of southern West Virginia. Wyoming County has a colorful history, a rich coal heritage, and beautiful scenery.

The first three permanent white settlers were all veterans of the American Revolution. John Cooke, his wife, and their four sons settled at present-day Oceana in 1799. Ralph Stewart and his family established their home a few miles from the Cookes. In 1802, Edward McDonald, his family, and son-in-law James Shannon settled in the Clear Fork Valley. The McDonalds built a plantation and were by far the wealthiest residents until the Civil War (1861–1865).

Wyoming County was formed from part of Logan County in 1850. The county's three incorporated towns have played important roles in the history and development of the area. Oceana served as the first county seat from 1850 to 1907. After several elections, the county seat was moved to Pineville, which is located in the center of the county. Mullens, a former major maintenance and repair facility of the Virginian Railway, became the marketing center and the county's largest town.

In the 19th century, most of the residents were farmers. Around 1890, logging became a significant economic activity. Logging remains an important activity, although its relative importance has declined. The Deepwater Railway, which reached Mullens in 1906, spearheaded the development of the county's rich coal veins. In 1907, the Virginian Railway assumed control of the Deepwater line. The railroad provided the means by which the mined coal could be transported across the county's rugged terrain to market. By 1912, commercial mines were operating, and in a few years, Wyoming County would become one of West Virginia's leading coal producing counties—a position it still maintains. After leading the country in coal production for many years, West Virginia currently ranks second.

Despite its relatively small size, Wyoming County (population 25,000 in 2000) has played important roles in West Virginia's history not only because of coal production but in political and athletic circles as well. Wyoming County has produced a large share of influential state government officials including Bill Marland, the state's 24th governor, and Judge R. D. Bailey. Wyoming County is also renowned for its rich sports history. There is no county in the country the size of Wyoming County that can match its long list of outstanding athletes and coaches.

Recently tourism and recreational activities have increasingly contributed to the county's economy. Twin Falls State Park is nestled in a beautiful mountain setting and is the showplace of the county. It features a wide array of accommodations and sporting and cultural programs. R. D. Bailey Lake is noted for its outdoor activities. In addition, the Coal Heritage Trail runs through Wyoming County and attracts visitors who are interested in seeing how coal influenced the social and cultural fabric of southern West Virginia.

In July 2001, much of southern West Virginia was devastated by a flood. Displaying an indomitable spirit when confronted with adversity, Wyoming Countians with strong resolve have rebuilt their homes, businesses, churches, and lives.

The following list includes some of the important events in the history of Wyoming County:

C. 10,000 B.C.–A.D. 1700. Native Americans inhabited the land that would become Wyoming County.

1780. Scout David Hughes led Edward McDonald to the Clear Fork Valley. McDonald surveyed the land.

1799. John Cooke and his family settled at Oceana.

1800. Ralph Stewart and his family settled at Crany. The first child of European descent, Juda Cooke, was born at Oceana.

1802. Edward McDonald and his family settled in the Clear Fork Valley. McDonald's son-in-law, James Shannon, established a nearby plantation at present-day Brenton. Other very early settlers in Wyoming Company included the Morgans, Baileys, and Lesters.

1812. Seven charter members organized the Guyandotte Baptist Church at Oceana.

1828. The post office department established a post office, Ginseng, at Oceana.

1840. Local residents organized a Methodist church at Sun Hill.

1850. Wyoming County was formed from Logan County. The county seat was established at Oceana. Formerly, the community was known as Cassville and Sumpterville.

1861–1865. Unlike several other southern West Virginia counties that were decidedly pro-South, the sympathies of Wyoming County residents were divided during the Civil War. While there were no major battles fought in the county, the home guards of both sides were active in Wyoming County.

1880–1917. Wyoming County had a bustling timber industry. Logs were floated down the Guyandotte River to market.

1906. Deepwater Railway reached Mullens. The name of the railroad was changed to Virginian Railway (VGN) the next year. W. M. Ritter established a large lumber operation at Maben.

1907. The county seat moved from Oceana to Pineville. Later in the year, Oceana suffered a fire that destroyed much of its business district.

1912. John C. Sullivan of Mullens opened the first commercial coal mine in Wyoming County.

1916. Workmen completed Wyoming County's impressive courthouse in Pineville.

1917. Fire destroyed much of the business district of Mullens.

1919. A fire in Mullens destroyed the portion of the business district that had been spared by the fire of 1917.

1920. The impressive coal company store at Itmann was completed.

1922. Glen Rogers Coal Mine was opened.

1933. Glen Rogers Mine produced 867,340 tons of coal, which ranked second in the state.

1938. Kopperston, America's model coal town, was created.

1959. VGN was acquired by the Norfolk and Western Railway (N&W).

1960. Glen Rogers Mine closed. Ritter Lumber Company was acquired by the Georgia-Pacific Lumber Company.

1970. The State opened Twin Falls State Park.

1980. The R. D. Bailey Dam was dedicated.

1982. Southern Railway and the N&W merged to form Norfolk Southern Railway.

2001. On July 8, Wyoming County suffered a devastating flood.

One

THE SETTING

This bird's-eye view of the community of Coal Mountain illustrates the setting of many Wyoming County towns. Due to the rough terrain and V-shaped valleys, there is not much available space for a large concentration of people. As a result, towns tend to be small, long, and very narrow. (Photograph courtesy of Roger Lester.)

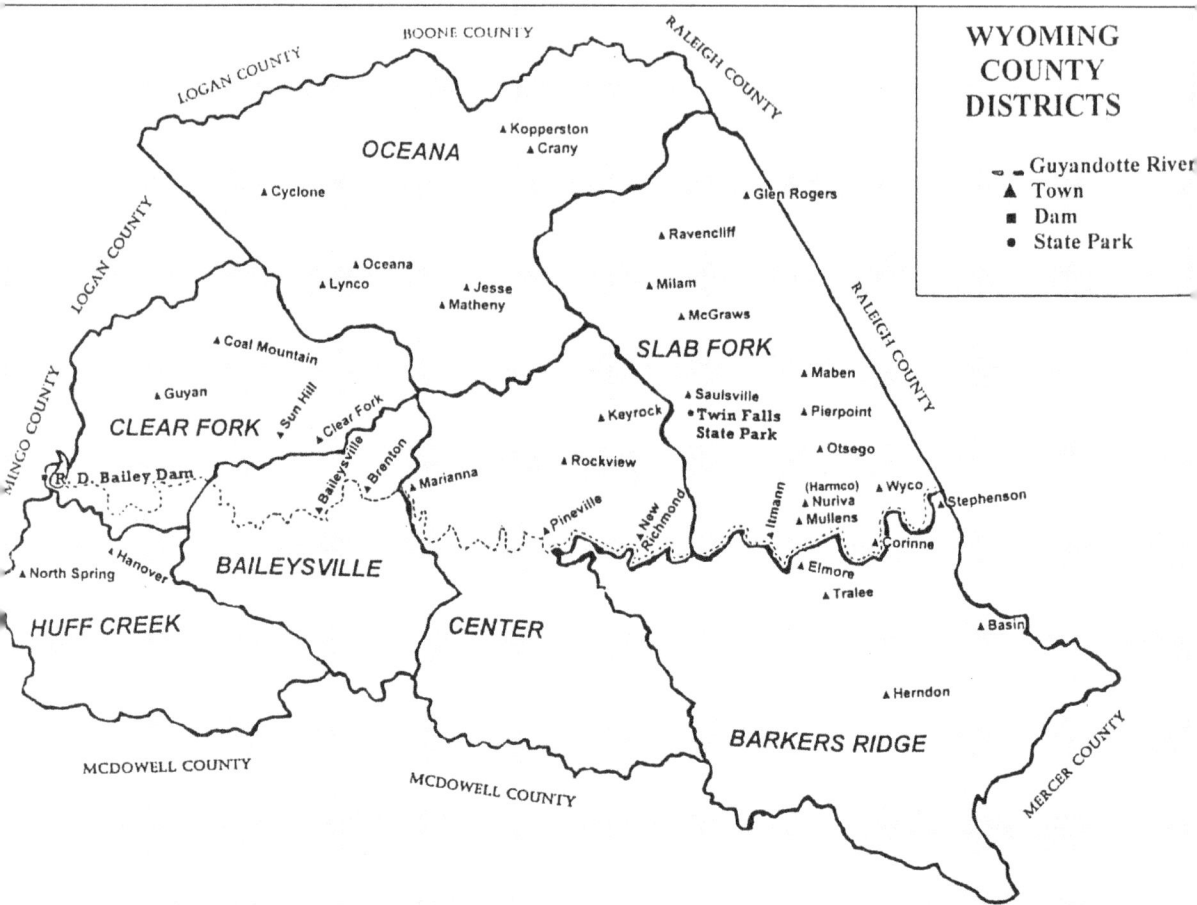

WYOMING COUNTY DISTRICTS

▪▪ Guyandotte River
▲ Town
■ Dam
● State Park

LOGAN COUNTY

BOONE COUNTY

RALEIGH COUNTY

OCEANA

▲ Kopperston
▲ Crany

▲ Cyclone

▲ Glen Rogers

▲ Ravencliff

LOGAN COUNTY

▲ Oceana
▲ Lynco

▲ Jesse
▲ Matheny

▲ Milam

▲ McGraws

RALEIGH COUNTY

MINGO COUNTY

▲ Coal Mountain

SLAB FORK

▲ Maben

▲ Guyan

Sun Hill ▲ Clear Fork

CLEAR FORK

▲ Saulsville
● Twin Falls State Park

▲ Keyrock

▲ Pierpoint

▲ Otsego

R. D. Bailey Dam

Baileysville Brenton

▲ Marianna

▲ Rockview

(Harmco)
▲ Nuriva
▲ Mullens

▲ Wyco
▲ Stephenson

▲ North Spring

▲ Hanover

BAILEYSVILLE

▲ Pineville

▲ New Richmond

Litmann

▲ Corinne

▲ Elmore

HUFF CREEK

CENTER

▲ Tralee

▲ Basin

▲ Herndon

BARKERS RIDGE

MERCER COUNTY

MCDOWELL COUNTY

MCDOWELL COUNTY

This map shows Wyoming County by districts, including the towns mentioned in this book. For the purposes of this book, the districts are grouped into three chapters. Chapter Six includes the town of Oceana as well as the Oceana and Clear Fork Districts. Chapter Seven covers the town of Pineville and the districts of Center, Baileysville, and Huff Creek. Chapter Eight includes the town of Mullens and the Barkers Ridge and Slab Fork Districts. The Guyandotte River flows across the entire county. (Map courtesy of Susan Robinson.)

In 1983, *Wonderful West Virginia* magazine published an article containing pictures of the Luther Elkins petroglyphs (rock drawings) near Lynco as well as an interpretation. Dr. Barry Fell, a retired Harvard University professor of marine biology, proclaimed the petroglyphs contained the Celtic Ogam script and that they were probably made between the sixth and eighth centuries A.D. According to Dr. Fell's decipherment, the petroglyphs tell the story of Christ's nativity in considerable detail. The article sparked a firestorm of controversy. While Dr. Fell has adherents to his interpretation, most archaeologists and linguists discount his account and point out shortcomings in his scholarship. They believe the rock carvings were made by Native Americans. They assert that if Old World people made the petroglyphs, confirmation should be found through the discovery of their artifacts in association with such carvings. None have been found to date. In contrast, Native Americans left numerous artifacts in the vicinity. (Photographs courtesy of Justin Stover.)

These two men, c. 1910, are enjoying the beautiful scenery of the Guyandotte River near Pineville. The Guyandotte River, a tributary of the Ohio River, is 166 miles in length. It rises in southwest Raleigh County and flows across Wyoming County and through the R. D. Bailey reservoir before turning northward. It enters the Ohio River near Huntington, West Virginia. In the late 19th and early 20th centuries, loggers used the Guyandotte River to float logs to market. (Photograph from the Robert R. Keller collection.)

July 8, 2001, is a date that many residents of Wyoming County will never forget. On that Sunday, almost 10 inches of rain fell in a few hours. The Guyandotte River and its tributaries flooded. In some places, the water was seven feet deep. The flood destroyed and damaged many homes, businesses, and churches. Some residents are still rebuilding their homes and lives. This photograph shows the impact of the flood on the main street of Oceana. (Photograph courtesy of Chris Chambers.)

12

Workers built a coffer dam before construction started on the R. D. Bailey Dam. The coffer dam diverted the Guyandotte River so that work on the major dam could commence. This group attended the dedication of the coffer dam. From left to right, they are unidentified, Congressman Ken Heckler, Sen. Jennings Randolph, R. D. Bailey II, Angela Bailey, Sen. Robert Byrd, and unidentified. Thousands of people attended the formal dam dedication in 1980 with Senator Byrd giving the keynote address. (Photograph courtesy of U.S. Army Corps of Engineers, R. D. Bailey Lake staff.)

This photograph shows work on a railroad tunnel that was relocated due to the construction of the R. D. Bailey Dam. The U.S. Army Corps of Engineers (USACE) spent almost a third of the cost of the dam on relocations of facilities. In all, USACE relocated 25 miles of railroad tracks, 4 tunnels, and 13 miles of roads. (Photograph courtesy of USACE, R. D. Bailey Lake staff.)

The Guyandotte River had a history of flooding, causing deaths and extensive property damage. Particularly hard hit were communities west of Wyoming County in Mingo and Logan Counties. USACE constructed the R. D. Bailey Dam to reduce flood damage. Workers started construction of the dam in 1974. The entire project cost $180 million. The dam, which sits on the Wyoming-Mingo county line, is 310 feet in height and contains 5.7 million cubic yards of rock, 6.4 million pounds of steel, and 240,000 bags of cement. The photograph above shows the dam while it was under construction; the image below is a current view of the dam. (Photographs courtesy of USACE, R. D. Bailey Lake staff, and Susan Robinson.)

Two

THE VIRGINIAN RAILWAY

This Virginian Railway Mallet locomotive is shown in a 1950 photograph near the coal-mining town of Harmco. The American Locomotive Company constructed the engine in 1923; it was rebuilt in 1937 and scrapped in 1954. (Courtesy of Lloyd Lewis, author of *The Virginian Era*; photograph by H. Reid.)

H. H. Rogers (1840–1909) was a capitalist, businessman, and philanthropist. He was an energetic man who amassed a fortune of more than $100 million. His final achievement was the Virginian Railway, which extended from the coalfields of southern West Virginia to Sewalls Point, a port near Norfolk, Virginia. The railroad was built according to Rogers's high standards. The VGN had a reputation of having the best route and the best equipment, making it highly profitable. Rogers was an enigma. On the one hand, he was a fierce businessman nicknamed "Hellhound Rogers." On the other hand, he was a generous philanthropist who helped his close friend, Samuel Clemens (Mark Twain), get his finances in order. Also, Rogers funded the college educations of Helen Keller and Booker T. Washington, and he contributed liberally to 100 colleges. The photograph above shows Rogers seated on the caboose. He is the second gentleman from the left. (Photograph courtesy of the Millicent Library of Fairhaven, Massachusetts.)

16

This map shows the West Virginia coalfields served by the VGN. The railroad issued this map in 1959, just before it was acquired by the N&W. The coal mines in Wyoming County are blocked on the map legend. The Wyoming County coal mines on the left on the map are in the Logan coalfield. The rest are in the Winding Gulf coalfield. (Map courtesy of Lloyd Lewis, author of *The Virginian Era*.)

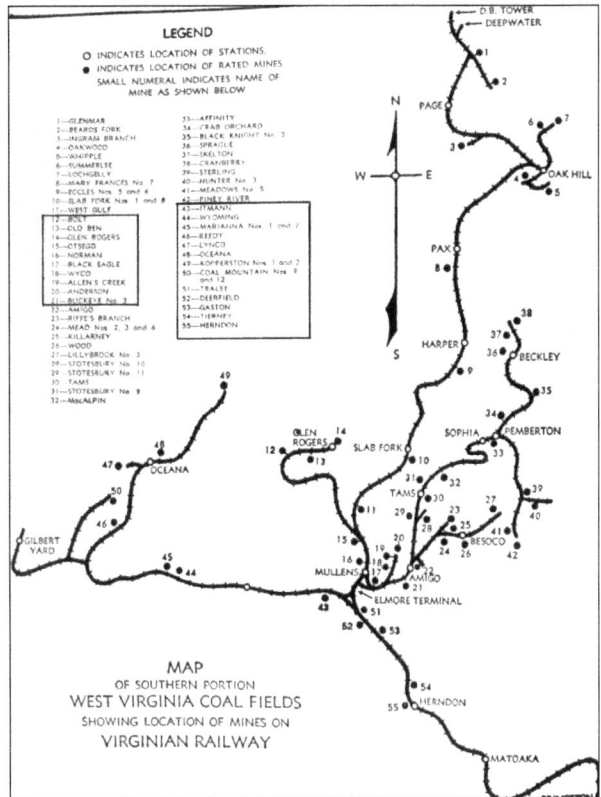

This photograph shows a Virginian Railway Mallet locomotive, which was named for the Swiss locomotive engineer and inventor, Anatole Mallet (1837–1919). Mallets were suited for service in Wyoming County's mountainous terrain. They produced twice the tractive power of an ordinary engine. In addition, they could negotiate curves better than other locomotives. The Mallet's principal drawback was that it could only be operated efficiently at low speeds. This disadvantage, however, did not adversely effect the Virginian's operations since it was primarily a freight carrier, and speed was not a prime consideration. (Photograph from the Robert R. Keller collection.)

Located two miles from Mullens, Elmore was a very important location for the Virginian Railway, because it was home to a car classification yard. In addition, steam locomotive maintenance and service was performed here as well as crew changes. This 1922 picture shows members of the shop crew. Shown left to right are William Stuhl, William Watson, H. S. Atkins, A. A. "Red" Akers, Floyd Bell, Samuel Barrett, Charles Stinnett, and Bernard Newsome. (Photograph courtesy of B. E. "Curley" Newsome Jr.)

The Virginian Railway was committed to massive equipment. Pictured here is the battleship gondola. These cars could hold 116 tons of coal, which was more than twice the capacity of the cars used by the Virginian's competitors. During the 1920–1924 period, the Virginian had more than 2,000 of these gondolas built. (Photograph courtesy of Lloyd Lewis, author *The Virginian Era*; photograph by H. Reid.)

James Sarver, third from the left, was the water boy for this 1916 road crew at Milam. Milam was located on a branch line of the Virginian. In 1932, the Virginian installed a 50,000-gallon water tank and a pump house at Milam. (Photograph courtesy of the Mullens Caboose Museum.)

In 1925, the VGN built this electric locomotive maintenance shop (Motor Barn) in Mullens. It was used in the repair of the large EL-class electric locomotives. The electric locomotives hauled coal and freight over the mountains to Roanoke, Virginia. Often, three shifts with 300 men worked at the Motor Barn. After the purchase of diesel locomotives during 1954–1957, the premises were used for repair and servicing. When the electric locomotives were discontinued in 1963 and diesel engine repair was moved to other locations, the Motor Barn was idle. (Photograph courtesy of the Eastern Regional Coal Archives [ERCA].)

Emerging from the Otsego tunnel is Engine 211, pulling a passenger train. The locomotive was built in 1920 and scrapped in 1957. Since the Virginian's prime objective was the hauling of coal, it never offered much passenger service. In 1950, the railroad had more than 15,000 freight cars and only 16 passenger cars. By 1956, it had ceased all passenger traffic due partly to the improvement of highways. (Courtesy of Lloyd Lewis, author of *The Virginian Era*; photograph by Richard J. Cook Sr.)

This 1951 photograph shows two Mallet locomotives pulling empty cars near Corinne on the Winding Gulf branch line. The Virginian and Chesapeake & Ohio railroads jointly served several mines in the hollows between Mullens and Beckley in Raleigh County, West Virginia. Tracks were laid on both sides of the river for about 15 miles, and each railroad granted the other trackage rights to get to jointly served coal mines. (Courtesy of Lloyd Lewis, author of *The Virginian Era*; photograph by S. K. Bolton, from the H. H. Harwood collection.)

Three

LOGGING AND COAL MINING

This locomotive is a Shay operated by the Ritter Lumber Company. Ritter established a large logging operation at Maben in 1906. Logging and coal mining have been the county's two major commercial industries. (Photograph courtesy of Shirley Blankenship Phillips.)

Logs on the Guyandotte River were a familiar sight in Wyoming County from the late 19th century to the early 20th. Loggers rafted the logs down the river because there were not any large lumber mills in the county to cut the timber. The promise of the railroad to build a line through Wyoming County encouraged W. M. Ritter to construct a large timber operation at Maben. (Photograph from the Robert R. Keller collection.)

The first commercial industry in Wyoming County was logging. The county had abundant stands of oak, poplar, hemlock, and chestnut trees. The lumbermen were confronted with a problem of transporting the timber because of the rugged terrain and the lack of adequate roads. A solution was splash dams. By releasing water behind several splash dams in a single watershed in a coordinated manner, a tide of water would be formed with sufficient force and volume to float logs downstream to market. Pictured here is a splash dam near the town of Crany. (Photograph courtesy of Barbara Keller.)

W. M. Ritter (1864–1952) came to southern West Virginia around 1900. With news of the railroad coming to Wyoming County, Ritter established a large lumber operation at Maben. His company grew to be one of the largest hardwood lumber producers in the world with extensive operations in eight states. During World War I, the president of the United States placed him on the Council of National Defense. Ritter was an advisor to five presidents. In 1960, the Ritter Lumber Company merged with the Georgia-Pacific Lumber Company. (Photograph courtesy of ERCA.)

This early-20th-century photograph shows Jeff Goode with a team of horses. Goode was a valued and trusted employee of the Ritter Lumber Company at Maben. (Maben was previously known as Estell, but VGN financier H. H. Rogers did not like that name and chose Maben in honor of a local landowner.) In 1929, the mill at Maben was the state's largest producer of hardwood lumber. (Photograph courtesy of Twin Falls State Park.)

This photograph shows a portion of the Ritter Lumber Company at Maben. Lumber from the mill was used to construct houses at several coal camps, including Itmann. On February 21, 1922, the Maben Mill broke its previous record by making a cut of more than 102,000 board feet. The same day, the Virginian transported 209,000 board feet of hardwood lumber from the Maben Mill. (Photograph courtesy of Shirley Blankenship Phillips.)

This photograph, taken around 1923, shows the Ritter Lumber Company planing mill crew at Maben. The Maben Planing Mill was well known for its fine strip flooring and parquet floors. In fact, some lumber experts regarded its floors as the best in the world. (Photograph courtesy of Twin Falls State Park.)

This attractive building was the Maben clubhouse. It featured a dining room and a large front porch. The community building had an assembly room, which, to the children's delight, showed movies. In 1915, Maben was a bustling town. In addition to the Ritter Lumber Company and clubhouse, the town had a railroad station, a community center, a post office, churches, five general stores, two hotels, a dry-goods store, a grocery store, a meat market, and a physician. (Photograph courtesy of Twin Falls State Park.)

This Shay locomotive of the Ritter Lumber Company is ready to haul its load of logs from Clear Fork to the mill at Maben. Ephraim Shay (1839–1916) of Ohio developed the Shay engine in 1878, and it was widely used for logging operations across the country. This locomotive was capable of delivering equal torque directly to the wheels on both sides at the same time. The Shay engine was particularly adept at negotiating a track bed with sharp curves and steep grades. (Photograph courtesy of Twin Falls State Park.)

Southern West Virginian coal miners have made significant contributions to the welfare and development of the United States. In 1998, this handsome black granite memorial was erected in their honor. The memorial is located at Twin Falls State Park. The inscription reads as follows:

In Memory of the Coal Miners of Southern West Virginia Who Perished from Mine Accidents or Lung Disease. May they rest in peace.

(Photograph by the author.)

Congressman Nick Rahall is shown here delivering the keynote address at the Virginian Rail Fans-Coalfields Seminar held at Twin Falls State Park in April 2005. In 1996, he introduced legislation that created the National Coal Heritage Area in southern West Virginia. The Coal Heritage Trail, designated in 1998 and located within the National Coal Heritage Area, encompasses five southern West Virginia counties, including Wyoming, and tells the story of the role of coal in the development of West Virginia. (Photograph by the author.)

Company coal towns such as Itmann, pictured here, were once prevalent in Wyoming County. Housing for the miners and their families was a necessity, and coal companies had the resources to provide housing. In 1922, 80 percent of miners in West Virginia lived in company towns. By the mid-1950s, company towns were far less common. The introduction of mechanization and technology advances in the mining industry, such as the mechanical cutting machine and the loading machine, sharply reduced mine employment. Also, there was increased surface mining, which required less manpower. (Photograph courtesy of Twin Falls State Park.)

Before the Glen Rogers Mine became the most productive mine in the county in the 1920s, the Itmann Mine held that distinction. In the late 1920s, the Itmann Mine closed, but it reopened two decades later. Itmann again became the county's largest mine. In 1961, the Itmann Mine produced a whopping 2.5 million tons of coal. This dramatic view of an N&W locomotive at the Itmann tipple was taken during the second era of Itmann mining operations. (Photograph courtesy of Pat Green Adams.)

It was not unusual for coal towns to have name changes. Traditionally the mine owner named the town, and a change of ownership was a fairly common practice. This community's name, however, changed more than most. It was first known as Trace Fork, named for the Trace Fork Coal Company, which was the original coal operator. The post office department rejected that name for the post office, and the name of Tracoal was adopted. Later the community would be known as Harmco and Nuriva. The company store is the building located in the center of the photograph near the small bridge. (Photograph courtesy of Twin Falls State Park.)

The company store was one of the most important buildings in a coal town. Company stores were virtual necessities because of the lack of commerce in coal-mining areas. Frequently the community's post office would be located in the company store. Residents would congregate at the company store to visit with friends or discuss the issues of the day. The photograph above shows, from left to right, Nell Jones, Jackie McGlothin, and Arlie Lafferty standing in front of the company store at Harmco (Nuriva) in the 1940s. (Photograph courtesy of Margaret J. Lafferty Lusk.)

This photograph shows the meat and produce department in the Glen Rogers Company Store. The grocers are Harley Christian (left) and Fred Manning. Hayden Wolfe, a Glen Rogers postmaster, once remarked, "Coal miners are a funny lot. They never had any money. But if a miner gets injured or killed, when the hat is passed around for the family, there was always several hundred dollars in it." (Photograph courtesy of Karl Lilly III and Bud Perry.)

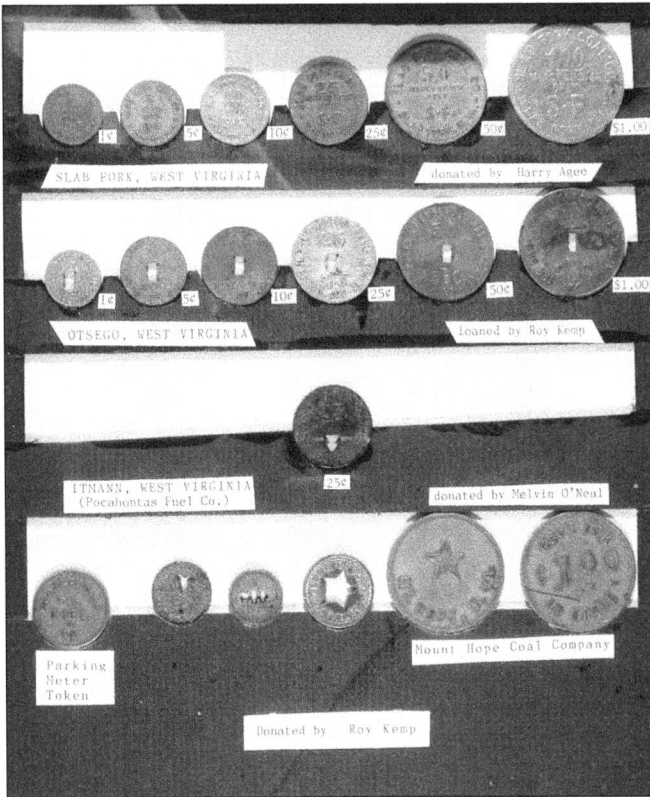

SLAB FORK, WEST VIRGINIA

donated by Harry Agee

OTSEGO, WEST VIRGINIA

loaned by Roy Kemp

ITMANN, WEST VIRGINIA
(Pocahontas Fuel Co.)

25¢

donated by Melvin O'Neal

Parking
Meter
Token

Mount Hope Coal Company

Donated by Roy Kemp

Coal companies issued part of coal miners' wages in the form of scrip for purchases in the company store. The scrip could only be used at that particular company store. This photograph shows scrip issued by coal companies at Slab Fork, Otsego, Itmann, and Mount Hope. Otsego and Itmann are in Wyoming County, while Slab Fork is in Raleigh County, and Mount Hope is in Fayette County. The picture below shows an ice coupon, which could be redeemed at the Glen Rogers Company Store. (Photograph of scrip courtesy of Roy Kemp; photograph of ice coupon courtesy of Twin Falls State Park.)

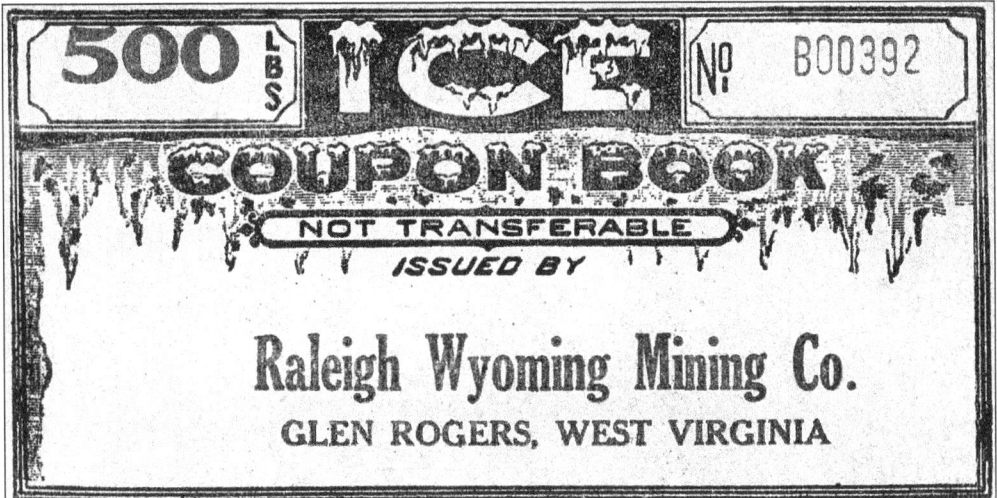

500 LBS ICE

Nº B00392

COUPON BOOK

NOT TRANSFERABLE

ISSUED BY

Raleigh Wyoming Mining Co.

GLEN ROGERS, WEST VIRGINIA

This photograph shows a miner at Harmco in the 1940s with a tester for gas over his shoulder and a lantern hanging from his belt. The expression "a picture is worth a thousand words" certainly applies to this photograph. One can imagine these thoughts floating in his head: he has been a coal miner for a long time. He is tired. Coal mining is a difficult and dangerous job. But his family needs food and clothes. He is determined to do his job and do it well. (Photograph courtesy of the National Archives, College Park, Maryland; Still Pictures, RG 245-MS-1102L.)

These Harmco miners trudge home on a dusty path after their morning shift. The houses shown in the photograph were typical for coal towns in the 1940s. Houses usually were of frame construction and were not insulated. Often the houses consisted of three or four rooms, and very few had indoor plumbing. In contrast, the mine superintendent's dwelling was commonly the largest in town and could range from 10 to 20 rooms. (Photograph courtesy of the National Archives, College Park, Maryland; Still Pictures, RG-245-MS-1797L.)

Because of their shared experiences in a challenging environment, coal miners often forge friendships and bonds with their coworkers that last a lifetime. Reunions of former miners are well attended. This photograph shows a reunion of Kopperston preparation plant retirees. Pictured, from left to right, are the following: (first row) unidentified, Bob Cuddy, unidentified, Richard Brewer, Fred Brooks, John Goddard, Ralph Hickman, Eidron Hamilton, and Jim Richardson; (second row) Eugene Singleton, G. W. Ford, Dewayne Shumate, Hobert Morgan, Chris Chambers, Luther Blankenship, Everett Blevens, Oscar Belcher, and Carlos Cook; (third row) unidentified, Jack Paynter, Bobby Hughes, Roscoe Morgan, Robert Thacker, Lonnie Marcum and U. J. Toler; (fourth row) Ray Stanley, Thomas Evans, Jack Walker, Jim Sigmon, Johnny Ball, Orville Lusk, Ed Hall, unidentified, Tom Rollins, Buren Lusk, and Ron Toler. (Photograph courtesy of Chris Chambers.)

The photograph above shows cars loaded with coal moving from the Harmco mine to the tipple. At the tipple, the coal will be dumped into railroad gondolas or hopper cars for shipment to market. A tipple is a processing structure for cleaning and sizing coal. Its name is derived from the act of tipping the coal onto the rail cars. Pictured below is the tipple at Kopperston. The buckets going up the hill are carrying slate for disposal. (Photographs courtesy of the National Archives, College Park, Maryland; Still Pictures, RG-245-MS-1842L and RG-245-MS-1659L.)

Unlike the children of today, with MP3 players, cell phones, and video games, boys and girls who lived in the early 20th century often had few toys and games. Shown here is a young boy, the son of a Harmco miner, quietly playing with his toy car beneath his home. In the background is the boy's wagon. (Photograph courtesy of the National Archives, College Park, Maryland; Still Pictures, RG-245-MS-1794L.)

In the 1940s, many coal towns did not have indoor plumbing. This young wife of a Harmco miner was fortunate. A former tenant had installed this tap in the home, and she did not have to go to the community pump to get water. An interesting feature of this picture is her reflection in the mirror. (Photograph courtesy of the National Archives, College Park, Maryland; Still Pictures, RG-245-MS-1811L.)

This vehicle is called a man trip. It transports miners to and from the working sections of an underground mine. (Photograph courtesy of the National Archives, College Park, Maryland; Still Pictures, RG-245-MS-1767.)

These Kopperston miners are waiting to check in at the lamp house after the completion of their shift. For many miners, mining and their coal town represented much of their lives—virtually from cradle to grave. The coal miners' lament can be expressed by the saying: "You could be baptized in the company church, educated in the company school, shop in the company store, play baseball for the company team, go to the company doctor when sick, and when you die, be buried in the company cemetery." (Photograph courtesy of the National Archives, College Park, Maryland; Still Pictures, RG-245-MS-1765L.)

Coal mining, particularly until the 1940s, was a very dangerous job. It also was very difficult. Fortunately for the miners shown in the above photograph, they had plenty of room to work. In some mines, the space was so cramped that the miner had to lie down in order to work a vein of coal. Even with increased mechanization, working in a coal mine was still a hazardous job. Woodrow Lamb (left) and Cyrus Williams are shown in the bottom photograph riveting a railroad frag onto a bedplate at the Kopperston machine shop. (Top photograph courtesy of the Eastern Regional Coal Archives; bottom photograph courtesy of the National Archives, College Park, Maryland; Still Pictures, RG-245-MS-1770L.)

Four

POLITICS AND
PATRIOTISM

John F. Kennedy campaigned for the presidency extensively throughout West Virginia and in Wyoming County in 1960. He is shown here in Mullens with Dr. Ward Wylie (center) and Franklin Roosevelt Jr. behind driver Margaret Hasli. Kennedy also visited Pineville and Oceana. (Photograph courtesy of Betty Wylie Farmer.)

As the population in the area increased, there was a growing desire to have a county seat that was closer to the residents. James Ferguson introduced legislation in 1849 to create a new county from the existing Logan County. The bill was swiftly passed in 1850. Ferguson inserted the name of Wyoming for the new county. His basis for choosing that name remains a mystery. Ferguson was Wyoming County's first commonwealth attorney. He later became an eminent judge. (Sketch courtesy of Paul Blankenship.)

In 1850, 14 gentlemen justices met in the home of John Cooke Jr. in Oceana to organize the government of the new county of Wyoming. The justices were as follows: John Cooke Jr. (1778–1858); James Pine Christian (1800–1892); James Cooke (1812–1879); Jacob Hatley Cook (1814–1898); James Shannon (1787–1881); Layne Shannon (1789–1865); Isaac Bailey (1800–1865); James Bailey (1806–1874); William McDonald (1793–1862); William Brooks (1795–1866); George B. Sizemore (1806–1866); Jordan McKinney; Thomas Godfrey; and John Howerton. This building in Oceana was the courthouse of Wyoming County from 1851 to 1907. (Photograph courtesy of Barbara Keller.)

Stella Swope, shown here in a 1910 photograph, was a daughter of J. J. Swope. The elder Swope (1854–1918) established the newspaper *Wyoming Mountaineer* in Oceana in 1904. When Swope was denied the purchase of some property in Oceana, he was furious. Subsequently, he moved his residence and the newspaper to Pineville. He made the newspaper's principal objective to be the removal of the county seat from Oceana to Pineville. His forceful editorials on this topic are credited by many historians as a main factor in Pineville finally winning the courthouse battle. (Photograph from the Robert R. Keller collection.)

Herndon M. Cline, postmaster, and Mamie Shawver, clerk, stand next to the Pineville Post Office in this 1908 photograph. It was common for the postmaster to be a very prominent person in the community, particularly in the late 19th and early 20th centuries. In fact, Cline served in the West Virginia House of Delegates in 1897. Other postmasters who also served in the state legislature and their respective post offices include the following: L. B. Chambers (Oceana); John McGraw (Joe's Branch, McGraws); A. J. Mullins (Mullens); and D. D. Moran (Mullens). (Photograph courtesy of Mike Goode.)

When the county seat was moved from Oceana to Pineville in 1907, county officials used the building shown in this photograph as the temporary courthouse. The photograph below presents the dedication ceremony of the beautiful permanent courthouse in 1916. The Judge R. D. Bailey House is next to the courthouse. (Top photograph from the Robert R. Keller collection; bottom photograph courtesy of Roger Lester.)

These imposing structures are the Wyoming County Courthouse, on the left, and the jail. The United States Department of the Interior has placed the structures on the National Register of Historic Places. The two-story courthouse is a Classic Revival structure of locally quarried stone. Workmen constructed the building in 1916. An interesting aspect of the courthouse is the Imperial Roman–style portico. The portico is carried by four Roman Tuscan columns. A handsome domed cupola is pierced by clock faces on all sides. Workmen completed the jail in 1929. It is made of the same locally quarried stone as the courthouse. The courthouse and jail sit on a two-acre hillside site in the center of Pineville. The courthouse square is enclosed by a stone wall and contains three wide, beautiful terraces. The impressive landscaping adds to the pleasing appearance of the courthouse complex. Further enhancing the overall effect of the area are the numerous monuments and memorials that dot the courthouse lawn. Few counties have done a better job than Wyoming in combining county administrative functions with county history in an aesthetically pleasing and informative manner. (Photograph courtesy of Pat Green Adams.)

After the death of W. H. H. Cook, R. D. Bailey and Frank Shannon (1883–1947) led the drive to erect a statue in honor of the beloved soldier, legislator, and minister. Ample funds were quickly received, and the statue was promptly erected on the courthouse steps. Bailey and Shannon made an interesting pair. Shannon was a brilliant courthouse orator. Citizens would flock to the courthouse to hear him litigate important cases. Shannon and Bailey were cousins, close friends, and law partners. Interestingly, Bailey was a stalwart of the Democratic Party while Shannon was a staunch Republican. (Photograph by the author.)

The bell that sits on the courthouse lawn has had an interesting travel history. In 1871, the bell was placed in the Oceana Courthouse tower. When the county seat was moved to Pineville in 1907, the bell was transported along with the county records. The temporary courthouse did not have a bell tower, and the court loaned the bell to a Pineville church. In the 1930s, the court placed the bell on the courthouse lawn. In the 1940s, the bell was loaned to a Kopperston church. It was returned to the courthouse lawn in 1973. (Photograph by the author.)

John McGraw is buried in the Pine Grove Baptist Church cemetery. During the Civil War, John McGraw (1824–1918) operated a large farm. He usually kept 200 sheep, 100 cattle, and many hogs, chickens, and horses. Both the Union and Confederate Home Guards raided his farm for livestock. In 1868, he established a post office and a store at Joe's Branch. In 1870 and 1878, he was elected to the West Virginia legislature. He opened a store at McGraws (now Ravencliff) in 1878 and also served as the first postmaster at McGraws. (Photograph courtesy of Susan Robinson.)

One of the most popular individuals who lived in Wyoming County was Rev. W. H. H. Cook (1840–1923). He affectionately was called "Little Harry" and "Preacher Harry." In 1861, he enrolled in the Confederate army. He had a change of view and later became a Union soldier. During his ministerial career, he served 15 churches, built seven houses of worship, and baptized 2,000 converts. In 1866, he was elected to the West Virginia House of Delegates, and in 1894, he was elected to the West Virginia Senate. (Photograph courtesy of Paul Blankenship.)

R. D. Bailey (1883–1961) was born in Baileysville and was a circuit court judge from 1920 to 1929. While a jurist, he gained a nationwide reputation for his clear thinking and ability. He presided over the trial of Clyde Beal, who was accused of murder. The jury found Beal guilty of murder in the first degree with no recommendation for mercy, which made the death sentence mandatory. Bailey was convinced that Beal was innocent. Bailey, in an unusual act, resigned rather than sentence Beal to death. On this matter, Bailey commented, "I would rather be right than judge." (Photograph courtesy of Christy Bailey.)

Like his father, R. D. "Bob" Bailey II (1912–1989) was born in Baileysville and became an attorney. From 1936 to 1961, he was either the assistant prosecuting attorney or the prosecuting attorney of Wyoming County. Bailey served as West Virginia secretary of state from 1965 to 1967. He was also very active in the Democratic Party. (Photograph courtesy of Christy Bailey.)

These three men were among the most influential and powerful in the history of Wyoming County. They are, from left to right, William "Bill" Marland, Judge R. D. Bailey, and J. W. Marland, Bill's father and the superintendent of the Glen Rogers Coal Mine. "Bill" Marland (1918–1963) was West Virginia's 24th governor, the only one who had been a coal miner. Marland skillfully handled school integration, brought new industry to the state, and fostered the state's excellent state park system. Shortly after entering office, he proposed a severance tax on the extraction of natural resources to the state legislature. The opposition to his tax plan was fierce; many claimed it would ruin the coal industry in West Virginia. Ultimately the proposal was shelved. Twenty years later, the state adopted a severance tax. In retrospect, even some of his loudest critics admitted that, in many aspects, Marland was ahead of his time. (Photograph courtesy of Mike Goode.)

Dr. Ward Wylie (1900–1970) was a gentleman of wide and diverse talents and interests. He was an athlete, physician, legislator, and sportsman. In college, he was captain of the West Virginia University wrestling team. He practiced medicine and operated the Wylie Hospital in Mullens. He was a close friend of John F. Kennedy. President Kennedy offered Wylie the prestigious post of surgeon general, but he declined the position since it would have required him to leave West Virginia. Wylie served in the West Virginia Senate for more than 20 years. He was elected president of the National Wrestling Association as well as the National Boxing Association. This picture shows him while he was serving as a captain in the Army Medical Corps during World War II. (Photographs courtesy of Betty Wylie Farmer.)

Citizens of Wyoming County have a high sense of patriotism, honor, and duty. When liberty and freedom have been challenged, they have been at the forefront in defending these rights. They have proudly served with distinction in all of the country's wars. Lt. William Patton was killed in the Battle of Bulge in Belgium on December 26, 1944. His medals included a Silver Star and two Purple Hearts. Patton was an outstanding athlete at Mullens High School and a 1943 graduate of Virginia Tech. (Photograph courtesy of Jack Feller.)

Lt. William P. Patton
K I A Belgium
December 26, 1944

PURPLE HEART

PURPLE HEART

106th DIVISION

SILVER STAR MEDAL

Captain Charles H. Feller
"Charlie"

Mullens, West Virginia

P-47D
"Double Trouble"

375th
Fighter
Squadron

361st
Fighter
Group

8th Air Force

1921 - 1944

Capt. Charles Feller was a P-47 Thunderbolt pilot and was credited with destroying two enemy aircraft. He and Lieutenant Patton were two of the county's most decorated heroes. Feller's honors included the Distinguished Flying Cross, two Air Medals for meritorious service, and a Purple Heart. He was killed in action on April 27, 1944. Feller was a student at West Virginia University before entering the service. (Photograph courtesy of Jack Feller.)

This picture was taken of Thurman and Recie Rinehart Miller on their wedding day in 1944. Thurman was a highly decorated Marine who saw action in major battles in the South Pacific theatre during World War II. After the war, Thurman worked at the mines at Otsego and Herndon for 35 years as a machinist and electrician. Recie worked at the company store at Otsego. Thurman has written two books chronicling his experiences in the military and coal mines. (Photograph courtesy of Thurman Miller.)

Sgt. James Richmond (1912–1980) of Mullens had a harrowing experience during World War II. He was a waist gunner on a B-24 bomber that was returning to base after a mission. Due to a severe storm, the crew parachuted at 12,000 feet over New Guinea. His landing was perilous, but he survived. Richmond and the rest of the crew then embarked on a seven-day hike to the ocean over some of the most difficult terrain in the world. Their ordeal was featured in the August 12, 1944, edition of the *Saturday Evening Post*. (Photograph courtesy of Sue Richmond.)

Outstanding athlete and coach Lewis D'Antoni saw extensive action in the navy during World War II. Lieutenant Junior Grade D'Antoni served 44 months, including 15 months at sea. His honors included the Philippine Liberation Medal with a bronze star, the Asiatic-Pacific Medal with three battle stars, and the American Defense Ribbon Citation. (Photograph courtesy of Lewis D'Antoni.)

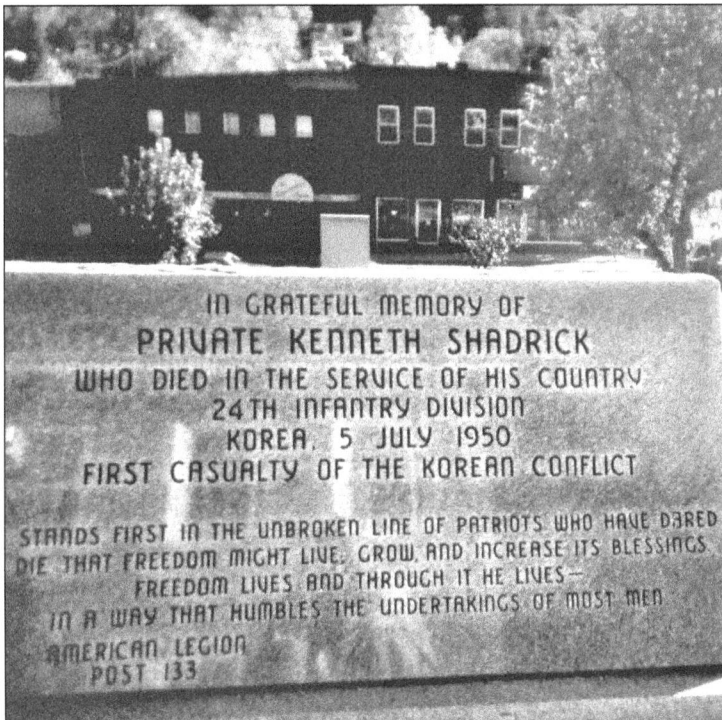

IN GRATEFUL MEMORY OF
PRIVATE KENNETH SHADRICK
WHO DIED IN THE SERVICE OF HIS COUNTRY
24TH INFANTRY DIVISION
KOREA, 5 JULY 1950
FIRST CASUALTY OF THE KOREAN CONFLICT

STANDS FIRST IN THE UNBROKEN LINE OF PATRIOTS WHO HAVE DARED
DIE THAT FREEDOM MIGHT LIVE, GROW, AND INCREASE ITS BLESSINGS
FREEDOM LIVES AND THROUGH IT HE LIVES—
IN A WAY THAT HUMBLES THE UNDERTAKINGS OF MOST MEN
AMERICAN LEGION
POST 133

Pvt. Kenneth Shadrick of Wyoming County was the first U.S. casualty of the Korean Conflict in June 1950. On the courthouse lawn, there is a memorial to Shadrick that reads as follows: "He stands first in the unbroken line of patriots who have dared to die that freedom might live, grow and increase its blessings. Freedom lives and through it he lives—in a way that humbles the undertakings of most men." (Photograph by the author.)

49

These well-dressed children assembled in the yard of Isaac B. Brooks with their wagons. They were preparing to parade down Main Street in Pineville. (Photograph from the Robert R. Keller collection.)

SMALL TOWNS ARE AN ATTITUDE

By Craig E. Sathoff

Yes, small towns are an attitude
Toward helping one another
Where each man finds a special joy
In making glad the other.

A small town thrives on kindly words
And kindly deeds to share
The essence of each day is this:
Capacity to care.

Yes, small towns are an attitude
Toward loving simple things
Like quilting bees and church bazaars
And Christmas carolings.

A small town thrives on hay rides
And programs in the park
And picknicking and school affairs
And bonfires before the game after dark.

The attitude is one of peace
From deeply thinking hearts
Who saw what deeds must be done
And gladly did their part.

(Poem courtesy of Mary Sathoff with thanks to Jack Feller.)

50

Five

SPORTS AND RECREATION

Before Lewis D'Antoni became a legendary coach at Mullens High School, he coached at Pineville High School. In fact, this 1937–1938 Pineville team defeated arch rival Mullens twice during the season. D'Antoni is shown here with the team. He is at the far right end of the third row. (Photograph courtesy of Lewis D'Antoni.)

In the early 20th century, one of the main sources of recreation for young boys in the summer was swimming. This *c.* 1910 photograph shows a group of boys enjoying the water at the Phlegar Hole of the Guyandotte River. It would be many more years before girls and women would swim here. (Photograph from the Robert R. Keller collection.)

Widy Shannon (left) and Waterson Gonley of the Pineville baseball team are shown in this *c.* 1910 photograph. During the first half of the 20th century, baseball was popular in the towns of southern West Virginia, particularly in the coal towns. Sunday-afternoon games were major social events. The quality of play was high with several players ultimately making the major leagues. After World War II, interest in baseball and its teams declined. Improved mechanization of coal mining reduced the number of coal miners and coal company teams. (Photograph from the Robert R. Keller collection.)

This 1985 Glen Rogers basketball team went to the state tournament and compiled a 20-5 record. The team was coached by Larry Stewart. Wyoming County girls basketball high school teams consistently produce strong squads. The 1991 Baileysville team advanced the furthest in the state tournament, losing in the finals. The Wyoming East team has gone to the state tournament seven consecutive years (1999–2005). (Photograph courtesy of Karl Lilly III and Bud Perry.)

Despite the lack of clarity, this 1950 photograph of the sixth grade Glen Rogers basketball team illustrates that children started playing organized and competitive basketball in Wyoming County at an early age. Pictured from left to right are coach John Lubich, Bobby Phylian, Tracy Accord, Jack Mosely, Leon Boulain, Don Nuckols, and principal Kelly Sizemore. Formerly coach Lubich was an outstanding football and basketball player at Glen Rogers High and Concord College. (Photograph courtesy of Don Nuckols.)

This 1935–1936 Glen Rogers basketball team went to the state tournament. Jim McNeish, third from the left on the front row, was the star. He was one of the best all-around athletes ever to play in Wyoming County. Since his school did not have a track team, McNeish hitchhiked to the state meet his junior and senior years. His junior year, he won the broad jump, and he placed second the next year. The great Olympics champion Jesse Owens barely beat McNeish in an exhibition 100-yard dash. (Photograph courtesy of Karl Lilly III and Bud Perry.)

Andy Botney, a 1934 graduate of Glen Rogers High School, was the first athlete in Wyoming County to receive a scholarship from a major out-of-state university. He is shown here in his football uniform at Purdue University. Andy was also one of the most versatile athletes that the county has produced. He excelled at football, baseball, basketball, and swimming. After college, Botney established the football program at Oceana High School and coached there for seven years. (Photograph courtesy of the Purdue University Sports Information Office.)

One of the first great athletes produced by Wyoming County was Lewis D'Antoni, an outstanding football, basketball, and baseball player. He starred at Mullens High School and Concord College in the 1930s. D'Antoni also was a successful basketball coach. At Mullens High School, his teams recorded six 20-win seasons during a seven-year span with his 1955 squad winning the state championship. D'Antoni was named to the West Virginia Sports Hall of Fame in 2004. Now in his 90s, D'Antoni continues to excel in sports. He consistently shoots less than his age on the golf course. (Photograph courtesy of Lewis D'Antoni.)

Pineville's Buzzy Wilkinson, shown here shooting, earned All-American honors at the University of Virginia during the 1954–1955 basketball season. He averaged 32.1 points a game, which is both a school record and an Atlantic Coast Conference (ACC) record. Wilkinson's career scoring average of 28.6 points a game is also a school and ACC record. The fact that Wilkinson attained this level of achievement 50 years ago and that it has not been equaled since is remarkable. (Photograph courtesy of the University of Virginia Athletic Media Relations.)

Willie Akers, a two-time All State basketball player, was an important cog in Mullens High School's march to its first state basketball championship in 1955. In college, Akers teamed together with the great Jerry West at West Virginia University to produce some powerhouse teams. They lost to California by a single point with a score of 71-70 in the 1959 national championship game. Akers was a highly successful high-school coach at Logan (West Virginia) High School, where he won four state boys basketball championships. (Photograph courtesy of the West Virginia University Athletic Archives.)

Oceana High School was noted for its strong athletic program. Shown here is the Indians' 1965 state championship basketball team. From left to right are (first row) Larry Cook, Larry Laxton, Joe Pendry, head coach Paul Greer, Benny Cook, and Elwood Pennington; (second row) manager Billy Harvey, assistant coach John Beckelheimer, principal Ronald Cook, Larry Perry, Larry Mathis, Carl "Tuffy" Fleenor, Greg Daniels, Randall Topping, Tommy Evans, statistician Ralph Hannah, manager Mike Cook, and team physician Dr. E. G. Shannon. Coach Greer also guided Oceana to the 1963 state championship. (Photograph courtesy of Paul Greer.)

Joe Pendry, an Oceana High School graduate, has been a football coach in the National Football League (NFL) for 18 years. Currently he is offensive line coach of the Houston Texans. Teams he has coached have made the NFL playoffs 11 times, including one Super Bowl. At Oceana High School, he was an All-State performer in football as well as basketball. He was a member of the 1965 Oceana state championship basketball team. This photograph shows Pendry when he was playing for West Virginia University. (Photograph courtesy of the West Virginia University Athletic Archives.)

In this photograph, Mullens High School coach Don Nuckols instructs three of his players on the 1969 team that recorded an outstanding 19-2 record. Shown here from left to right are Jimmy York, Coach Nuckols, Carlos Hatfield, and Mike D'Antoni. Coach Nuckols was a member of a powerful Glen Rogers quintet in 1956, which scored 125 points in a game. Nuckols coached at Mullens High for 16 years, compiling an impressive 276-110 record. His teams won state titles in 1970, 1972, 1982, 1983, and 1984. (Photograph courtesy of Lewis D'Antoni.)

One of the saddest days in American sports was November 14, 1970. That was the day that a jet plane carrying the Marshall University football team and coaches crashed while returning to West Virginia after a game with East Carolina. All aboard were killed. The head coach was Rick Tolley, a former star athlete at Mullens High School. He is pictured above in the front row (the fourth coach from the left). Mullens High School placed a monument on their athletic field honoring Tolley. (Photograph courtesy of the Marshall University Athletic Media Relations.)

Greg White is the all-time assist leader at Mullens High School and Marshall University. In 1977, his senior year at Mullens, White averaged 24 points a game and over nine assists a game. He was head basketball coach at Marshall for seven years, and previously he was an assistant coach at UCLA. Currently, White is head coach at the University of Charleston, West Virginia. (Photograph courtesy of Marshall University Athletic Media Relations.)

One of the greatest athletes ever to come out of the state of West Virginia was Pineville High School's Curt Warner. He excelled at every level in football, and was an All-State performer in baseball and basketball in high school. He was also an outstanding student. Warner was West Virginia's amateur athlete of the year in 1978 and the recipient in the same year of the Kennedy Award, given to the best high school football player in the state. He is the state's all time career scoring leader on the gridiron with 577 points. In college, he was an All-American performer at Penn State University, leading the Nittany Lions to their first national title in 1982. Warner holds 41 Penn State football records. In the National Football League, Warner rushed for more than 1,000 yards four seasons during his professional career. He is a member of the Seattle Seahawks' Ring of Honor. (Photograph courtesy of Pineville High School Alumni Association, with thanks to David Stover.)

Mike D'Antoni, coach of the Phoenix Suns in the National Basketball Association (NBA), was named 2005 Coach of the Year. His team compiled a league best 62-20 record. At Mullens High School, he was a two-time All-State player. He graduated from Marshall University in 1973 as the school's all-time assist leader. D'Antoni played four seasons in the NBA. He spent the next 20 years as a star player and coach in the Italian professional league. (Photograph courtesy of the Marshall University Athletic Media Relations.)

Shawn Finney was another on the long list of outstanding Mullens High School basketball players. He was an assistant coach of the 1998 University of Kentucky national championship team and was the head basketball coach of Tulane University for five years. (Photograph courtesy of Tulane University Media Relations.)

60

This group of four talented basketball coaches combined to win seven state basketball titles. They are, from left to right, Lewis D'Antoni, Don Nuckols, Leonard Valentine, and Jim Pauley. D'Antoni and Valentine each won a state title, while Nuckols captured five state crowns. A Wyoming County bridge was named in honor of the beloved coach Valentine. Pauley was an assistant coach on Nuckols's 1982 and 1983 state championship teams. (Photograph courtesy of Don Nuckols.)

The annual Bear Hole Run, established in 1983, is held at Twin Falls State Park. The event attracts runners from a wide geographical area. Pictured is Gord Baldwin of Ottawa, Canada, with family and friends. They are, from left to right, Baldwin, Marlene Baldwin, Ed Robinson, Mark Baldwin, Ian Baldwin, Susan Robinson, and Anjuli Baldwin. Gord has run hundreds of different courses in North America and Europe. He regards the Bear Hole course as one of the most challenging as well as one of the most beautiful he has experienced. (Photograph courtesy of Gord Baldwin.)

The R. D. Bailey Dam created the 19,000-acre R. D. Bailey Lake, which is entirely in Wyoming County. The lake improves downstream water quality and provides fish and wildlife habitat and numerous recreational opportunities. Above is a picture of the Bailey Lake marina. The photograph to the left shows two young men standing in front of the visitor center proudly displaying their catch of catfish. The visitor center contains interesting exhibits regarding the dam, and it affords a spectacular view of the dam and the Guyandotte River Valley. (Photographs courtesy of USACE, R. D. Bailey Lake staff.)

Six

OCEANA AND VICINITY

This road surveying crew is taking a break from their chores. They are relaxing next to the John Cooke Sr. cabin in Oceana, which was constructed in 1799. Workers tore down the structure in 1922, shortly after this photograph was taken. (Photograph courtesy of Paul Blankenship.)

Shown here are two views of the John Cooke Sr. cabin. John Sr. (1752–1832) of London and his future wife, Nellie Pemberton of Scotland, were kidnapped while on a ship in London harbor. They arrived in America in 1766 and became indentured servants to a Virginia planter. After they completed their servitude, John and Nellie married and settled in the Shenandoah Valley of Virginia. John fought two years with the colonists in the Revolutionary War and received land grants for his military service. They settled in Oceana with their four sons (John Jr., William, Thomas, and James). Most historians regard Cooke as the first permanent settler of European descent in Wyoming County. (Photographs from the Robert R. Keller collection.)

Thomas and Ellen Cooke (1784–1850) were parents of 11 children. (On the plaque, their name is spelled Cook. Over the years, many family members dropped the "e" from the original name.) Ellen was a serious and deeply religious woman. She was a charter member of Guyandotte Baptist Church and the driving force in the establishment of the church. Thomas was a renowned fighter. He also was not averse to having a good time. (Photograph courtesy of Paul Blankenship.)

L. B. Chambers (1824–1892) was a business and political leader of Wyoming County. He established a store in a log cabin at Clear Fork in 1845. Around 1850, he moved to Oceana and built the first store and hotel there. He served as the first clerk of the Wyoming County Court. In 1884, Chambers was elected to the West Virginia House of Delegates. Thomas Dunn English, a poet, physician, and politician, suggested the name of Oceana for the community. The name is in honor of Shawnee chief Cornstalk's youngest daughter. (Portrait courtesy of Barbara Keller.)

65

A historic site in Wyoming County is this tree, the Old Baptist Beech. This place was the location of the home of Ellen Riggins Cooke and Thomas Cooke, John Sr.'s eldest son. Seven residents organized in 1812 the first church in the county, the Guyandotte Baptist Church, under the sheltering limbs of the old beech tree. Wyoming County's first post office, Ginseng, was established in 1828 and, for a time, was located in the home of Thomas and Ellen Cooke. (Photograph courtesy of Paul Blankenship.)

The charter members of the Guyandotte Baptist Church were Ellen Riggins Cooke, David Morgan, Catherine Stewart Cooke, William Cooke, Daniel Shumate, Samuel Morgan, and Capt. Ralph Stewart. Green Cooke, a member of the church, donated a parcel of land, and the congregation erected the church building in 1895 at Jesse. One of the early pastors of the church was W. H. H. Cook. (Photograph by the author.)

Rev. Bubba Salton, a circuit riding preacher, preached at the Delilah Chapel, which is located on part of the original John Cooke Sr. homestead in Oceana. John Sr., his wife Nellie, their son William, and his wife Catherine Stewart Cooke are buried in the churchyard. A local legend maintains that the ghost of John Sr. walks the halls of the church at midnight on the seventh day of the month. None of the church's present congregation has attempted to verify the accuracy of the legend. (Photograph courtesy of the Delilah United Methodist Church.)

Catherine "Kate" Stewart (1790–1888) was the eldest daughter of Ralph and Mary Clay Stewart. She married William Cooke (1784–1853), son of John Cooke Sr., in 1806. William Cooke is referred to as the "Father of Oceana." He donated the land for the first Wyoming County Courthouse. Everyone who met Kate admired her for her bravery and courage. When Native Americans attacked her half-brother while they were living in Kentucky, she is credited with saving his life, although she was just a small child. Kate and William were charter members of the Guyandotte Baptist Church. (Portrait courtesy of Paul Blankenship.)

This building was the second Oceana District High School from 1925 to 1951. After a new high school was built, this structure housed the Wyoming County Opportunity Council. (Photograph courtesy of Paul Blankenship.)

Under the leadership of Rev. Al Matheny, this frame church was built c. 1891, and it served the congregation for more than 50 years. The Matheny United Methodist Church was named for the pastor, and the community also became known as Matheny. Members of the Stewart family were prominent early members. Four sons of George P. Stewart planted sycamore trees at the four corners of the church property. (Photograph courtesy of Paul Blankenship.)

One of the most impressive houses of Wyoming County was the home of Franklin Pierce Roach (1858–1901) and his wife, Demaris. This Victorian home was completed in 1890 and featured 45 windows. Nina and Emma, daughters of Franklin and Demaris, lived in this home. The photograph below left shows Nina. The image below right is of Emma with the white blouse and a friend enjoying sticks of candy. Emma graduated from Oceana High School in 1912 and was the first high-school graduate of Wyoming County. (Photographs from the Robert R. Keller collection.)

Capt. Ralph Stewart (1749–1835) was born in Augusta County, Virginia. Stewart saw extensive action in the Revolutionary War. He was at Yorktown when Lord Cornwallis surrendered. During the war, Stewart suffered a saber wound from the British officer Lord Tarleton. Stewart married Mary Elliott. After she died, he married Mary Clay, the young daughter of Mitchell and Phoebe Clay of Mercer County (West Virginia) in 1788. They moved to present-day Wyoming County in 1800, settling at Crany. Stewart fathered 20 children. (Photograph courtesy of Jean Walker Lusk.)

Ottway Gunnoe served as principal of Oceana High School in 1912–1913. He then moved to Fayette County (West Virginia) where he eventually became the superintendent of schools. In addition to his work in education, he was a published poet. Many of the poems in his book *Homey Poems* recall his childhood days growing up in Crany. (Photograph from the Robert R. Keller collection.)

Pictured here are Edna Cook Brown and Elery Brown (1900–1938) with their son, James Dennis Brown. Elery was a preacher and worked at the Kopperston Mine. He was the first miner killed at Kopperston. (Portrait courtesy of Jean Walker Lusk.)

In the late 19th and early 20th centuries, Crany was one of the more important communities in the county. It was the ancestral home of many prominent families including the Stewart, Canterbury, Gunnoe, Marshall, Brooks, Lamb, and Roach families. The Reverend James Marshall, a resident of Crany, organized the Crany Baptist Church in 1886. This photograph shows four members of the Sunday school. They are, from left to right, Jean Walker, Della Wikle, Dollie Lamb, and Clara Kennedy. (Photograph courtesy of Jean Walker Lusk.)

71

The Crany area in the late 19th and early 20th centuries was noted for farming and logging. The photograph at left shows Jefferson Davis Cook (1861–1941) and his wife, Mary Ellen "Mollie" Brooks Cook (1861–1943). The image below is a photograph of their picturesque farm. Crany was the site of the first free school in the county (1820) and one of the first post offices (1856). Crany derived its name from the fact that a crane, a bird uncommon in the region, was spotted in the area. (Photographs courtesy of Jean Walker Lusk.)

Molasses making has been a popular activity in Wyoming County for many years. This early-20th-century photograph took place at the George Canterbury farm at Crany. Members of this group are, from left to right, as follows: (first row) Ethel Canterbury, George Sanders, Lightburn Canterbury, Mamie Stennett, Lilly Stennett (baby), Sola Canterbury, Okey Brooks, Martha Stennett, Cora Stennett, and Nida Canterbury; (second row) Fountain Canterbury, Fred Canterbury (baby), Becky Brooks (holding cane stalks to feed the mill), Mamie Stennett, and Oather Stennett (baby); (third row) Susan Cook Canterbury, George Canterbury, Maude Canterbury, Ed Stennett, Oliver Canterbury, and India Cook. (Photograph courtesy of Barbara Keller.)

The town of Cyclone received its name as a result of a severe cyclone that blew down trees in an area 300 yards wide and 600 yards long in 1887. When the post office department established a post office later that same year, the name of Cyclone was selected. Due to its unusual name, Cyclone made *Ripley's Believe It Not* on two occasions—in 1950 and in 1952. This drawing is the 1952 cartoon. (Cartoon courtesy of Ripley Entertainment, Inc., copyright 2005.)

Reed Cook (1818–1887) operated a gristmill in Cyclone. Gristmills were an important part of the economy of small towns and farming communities in the 19th and early 20th centuries. This old photograph shows Reed and his family at his home. Pictured on the porch, from left to right, are granddaughter Ruth, Reed, his wife Sarah (1848–1925), grandson Butch, and daughter Mary. On the balcony, from left to right, are sons Anthony and Grover. (Photograph courtesy of Chris Chambers.)

This photograph shows the 1948–1949 class of the Road Branch School. Pictured, from left to right, are (first row) Edgar Kennedy, Gary Browning, Joe Lee Osborne, Ann Cook, Jeanna Elkins, Bobby Carpenter, unidentified, Sue Elkins, unidentified, Leona May Workman, Carolyn Jeffrey, Paul Rollins, Ruby Lusk, Jerry Cobb, and Lanta Lusk; (second row) Jim Toler, Edwin Brown, Jerry Canterbury, Arvis Toler, David Cobb, Glen Browning, Gene Blankenship, unidentified, Dewayne Brown, Troy Brown, Bill Lusk, Shirley Cook, and Mary Blankenship; (third row) Helen Bane (teacher), Otis Bailey, Denver Murphy, Roger Murphy, unidentified, James Blankenship, Shirley Lusk, unidentified, Brookie Bailey, Minnie Lusk, Jean Kennedy, Lois Smith, Brookie Murray, and Marshall Bailey. (Photograph courtesy of Chris Chambers.)

This 1932 photograph shows Alva Cook, on the left, and his father, Buddy Cook, standing in front of Alva's garage. The garage was in Cyclone. (Photograph courtesy of Chris Chambers.)

Koppers Coal Company founded Kopperston in 1938. The community received national recognition as the country's model coal camp because of the excellent facilities and close cooperation between the company and miners. Facilities in the town included a church, doctor's office, grade school, community store, and a boarding house. The town was composed of more than 350 houses that had alternating roofs of red, green, and blue. This photograph shows a group of attractive houses with well-maintained lawns and concrete sidewalks. (Photograph courtesy of the National Archives, College Park, Maryland; Still Pictures, RG-245-MS-1621L.)

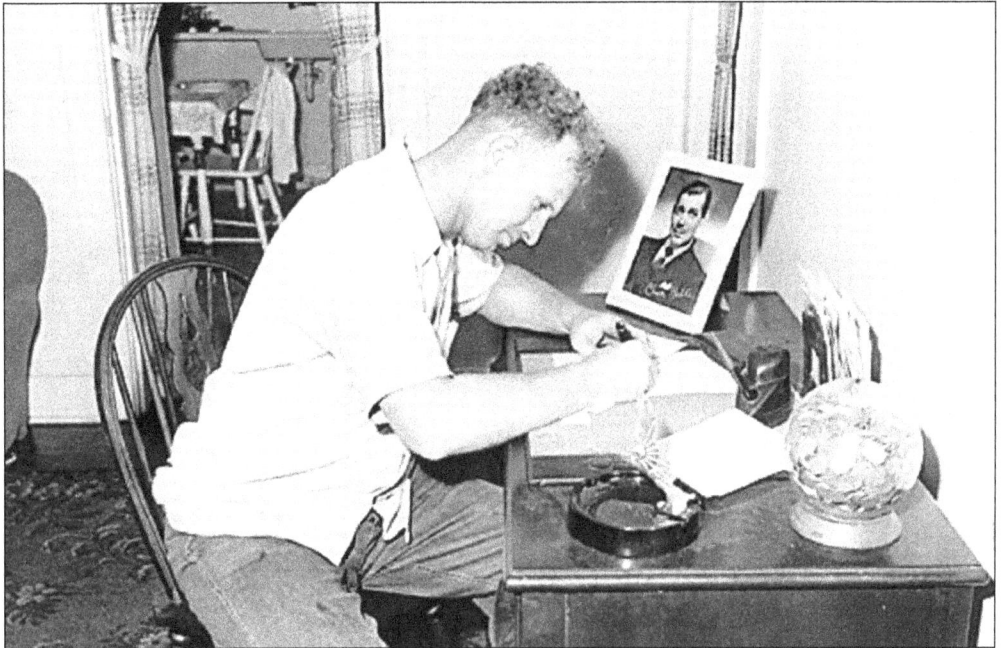

James Jasper, a motor brakeman at Kopperston, writes a letter to his parents in this 1946 photograph. Notice the picture of movie star Clark Gable on the desk. Jasper lived in the Kopperston company housing project with his wife and three young sons. (Photograph courtesy of the National Archives, College Park, Maryland; Still Pictures, RG-245-MS-1752L.)

These young boys, the sons of Kopperston miners, congregate at one of their favorite hangouts—the company-owned soda fountain. One wonders what they were talking about so intently. Are they discussing the latest cowboy movie or tomorrow's baseball game or . . . girls? It probably is not so difficult to determine what these young girls are talking about while playing with the toy house at the company store. (Photographs courtesy of the National Archives, College Park, Maryland; Still Pictures, RG-245-MS-1772L [above] and 1771L [below].)

Often an outsider's traditional view of coal camp life was that it was drab and uneventful. This outlook certainly was not always the case. This photograph shows the children of Kopperston miners enjoying summer camp at Camp Thomas E. Lightfoot in Summers County. The campers are in the dining hall singing a song that is being acted out. (Photograph courtesy of the National Archives, College Park, Maryland; Still Pictures, RG-245-MS-1705L.)

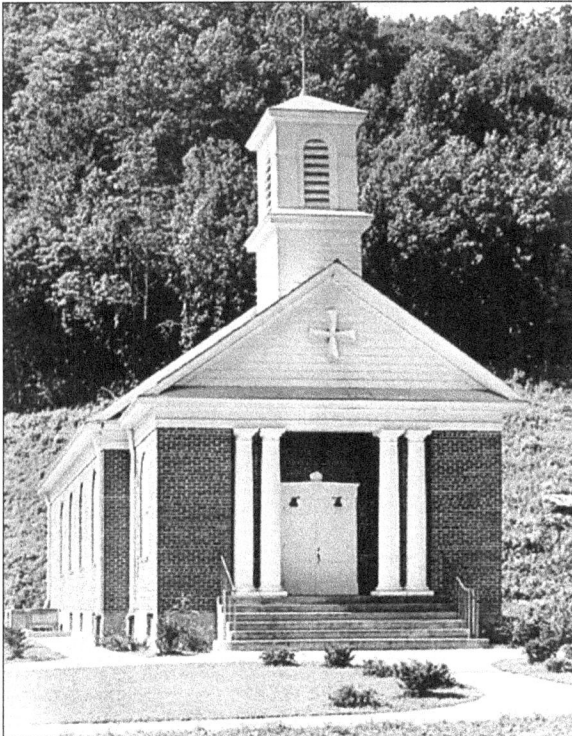

The Kopperston Church was organized in 1940. The operator of the coal mines, the Eastern Gas and Fuel Association, started construction of the church in 1944. For several years, the church was non-denominational, which was typical of coal camp churches, but in 1954, members of the congregation voted to join the Bluestone Presbytery. The bell, which now rests on the courthouse lawn in Pineville, graced the belfry of this church for about 25 years. (Photograph courtesy of the National Archives, College Park, Maryland; Still Pictures, RG-245-MS-1635L.)

Capt. Edward McDonald (1761–1835) was one of seven brothers who fought during the American Revolution. In the 1780s, he had surveyed the lands called the Big Bottoms, and he moved there with his family in 1802. Through the years, with a series of land grants, the McDonalds amassed property of 7,000 acres in the area. Prior to the Civil War, the McDonalds were the largest landowners in the county and easily the wealthiest family in the county. The McDonalds were staunch Confederate sympathizers, which made their plantation a prime target for Union soldiers. Their plantation was burned and destroyed in 1862 and never rebuilt. E. H. Crouch (1876–1955), in the 1930s and 1940s, acquired most of the land of the former McDonald plantation. On this property, he operated a large lumber company and a farm. The Crouch Lumber Company employed more than 50 people and produced 100,000 feet of lumber per week. Recently workmen demolished this barn during the construction of the Westside High School complex. (Photograph courtesy of Epp Cline.)

Sun Hill was primarily a farming community. The picture shows Epp Cole and his family in the 1920s. They are, from left to right, Epp holding Ethel, Virgi, Bessie holding Trudy, Masil (standing), and sitting are Ray and Troy. Later Ray ran a general store and Masil farmed. Troy passed away in the 1930s. On his farm, Epp grew vegetables and raised cattle. (Photograph courtesy of Epp Cline.)

Friends Mabel Toler Belcher and Virgi Cole share a hug. In the background is the historic Sun Hill Methodist Church that was built in 1897. The organization of the church dates back much earlier. Methodist minister Rev. Layne Shannon (1791–1865), one of the 14 justices who organized the county, built a log-cabin church on his land around 1840. (Photograph courtesy of Juanita Cook.)

The photograph above shows the Clear Fork Church of God. The church was established by Charley Blankenship around 1920 and was the first of that denomination in Wyoming County. The structure is still standing but is no longer in use. Matilda Jean Hatfield Miller, pictured below, was a niece of "Devil Anse" Hatfield, the leader of the Hatfield clan in the long-standing Hatfield-McCoy feud. She was an early member of the Clear Fork church. (Photographs courtesy of Dorothy Miller Green.)

This fine large house was the home of Sanford and Susan Meadows Morgan of Guyan. Builders constructed the house in 1915. It burned in the 1940s. Morgan was a merchant and a large landowner with extensive stands of timber. This photograph shows Susan Morgan with their children. They are pictured from left to right as follows: (seated) Josie, Vida, Ocie (behind Vida), Tollison Virgil, Cecilia, and Bessie; (standing) Susan and Lettie. (Photograph courtesy of Roger Lester.)

Guyan was once a thriving community with four general stores, a logging operation, restaurant, and hotel. The town no longer exists. Its residents had to leave due to the construction of the R. D. Bailey Dam and the creation of the lake. This 1940s picture shows Essie Perry Morgan in front of the Guyan Grill. She managed the grill, which was a popular spot for many years. (Photograph courtesy of Roger Lester.)

William Lester, a Revolutionary War soldier, was an early settler of present-day Wyoming County. Lester, a farmer, settled in the Coal Mountain area around 1800. William Lester is the progenitor of the numerous Lesters of Wyoming County. (Portrait courtesy of Roger Lester.)

Shown in this c. 1930 photograph are two residents of Coal Mountain, James "Doc" Perry, on the left, and the Reverend Eli Morgan. Both gentlemen were Confederate veterans of the Civil War. Doc was an herb doctor and the reverend was one of the founders of the Big Cub Missionary Baptist Church of Coal Mountain in the late 1890s. (Photograph courtesy of Roger Lester.)

Love of music has been a long-standing tradition of residents of Wyoming County. This 1920 photograph shows Bertie Lester (1902–1977) playing his handmade banjo. Lester was a union organizer for the United Mine Workers. He also was a Baptist pastor for more than 40 years. (Photograph courtesy of Roger Lester.)

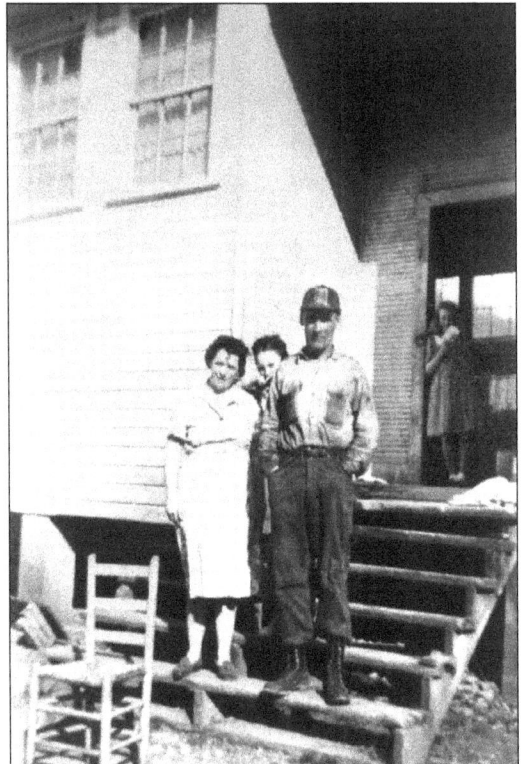

This 1940s photograph shows the building that was once the third elementary school in Coal Mountain. Claudia Hatfield later used the building as a home. Pictured, from left to right, are Doris Mitchell, Ollie Mitchell, and Harve Mitchell. On the porch is Dollie Hatfield. (Photograph courtesy of Roger Lester.)

Seven

PINEVILLE AND VICINITY

Five people standing on a foot bridge over the Guyandotte River near Pineville are shown in this c. 1910 image. While there are a number of modern bridges spanning bodies of water in the county, foot bridges are still in use. (Photograph from the Robert R. Keller collection.)

This *c.* 1908 photograph shows a picturesque view of Pineville. The 165-foot rock formation, Castle Rock, is visible next to the Guyandotte River on the left side of the picture. The Pineville area was settled first by Thomas M. Cook around 1840. After a number of unsuccessful elections, Pineville finally wrestled the county seat from Oceana in 1907. (Photograph courtesy of Twin Falls State Park.)

This *c.* 1910 picture shows the impressive rock formation known as Castle Rock that overlooks the town of Pineville. Castle Rock, a massive sandstone tower, was created by erosion of the Guyandotte River over a span of millions of years. Early residents loved to climb up Castle Rock. To facilitate the ascent, a resident placed a ladder at the base of the rock formation. One warm Sunday afternoon in 1907, a young man and his lady climbed Castle Rock. A prankster then removed the ladder. They were marooned for hours. (Photograph from the Robert R. Keller collection.)

The Robert and Mary Luella Keller family was one of Wyoming County's most prominent families in the 20th century. Family members, shown here from left to right, are (first row) Mary Luella Wright Keller, Nina Roach Keller and Eloise, Harry T. Hall and children, and Robert Alton Keller; (second row) Claude Keller (son), Kate Keller Hall (daughter), Mary Keller Bowman (daughter), Marvin T. Bowman, Ada Keller, and Robert R. Keller (son). Mary Luella Wright Keller was a teacher and postmaster in Nebraska before they moved to Pineville in 1899. The town of Luella, Nebraska, is named for her. Nina Roach Keller was a member of the well-known Roach family of Oceana. Robert Alton Keller was a business and civic leader. Mary Keller Bowman authored the first book of Wyoming County history, *Reference Book of Wyoming County History*. Her husband, Marvin T. Bowman, was an attorney. Robert R. Keller was the photographer whose pictures are featured in this book. (Photograph courtesy of West Virginia State Archives, Robert R. Keller collection.)

Robert R. Keller operated a photography studio in Pineville from 1910 to 1914. This photograph shows four men standing near Keller's business shingle. Pictured from left to right, they are Sheriff Charley Short, two unidentified men, and Robert R. Keller. A local newspaper article directed prospective customers to go to Robert R. Keller's studio for postcards, postcard hangers, suspension rings, flower pots, wall mottoes, flashlights, flashlight batteries, postcard albums, photograph albums, film, and film processing. (Photograph from the Robert R. Keller collection.)

As his fiancée, Nellie Ruth Hoover, looks on, Robert R. Keller carves their initials on a tree. Both of them loved the outdoors. Nellie Ruth often assisted Robert with his photographic endeavors. She was an accomplished musician. She was a fine pianist and had an operatic-quality voice. (Photograph from the Robert R. Keller collection.)

Rev. G. P. Goode (1868–1957) was a man of rare talent and dedication. This photograph shows him on horseback at the courthouse in Pineville. Many of his associations and commitments spanned decades. For more than 40 years, Goode was pastor of various county churches; he taught school for 44 years, was clerk of the Rockcastle Baptist Church for 40 years, served as county historian for 33 years, and was a speaker at the Cook family reunion for more than 20 years. (Photographs courtesy of Mike Goode.)

Mary Keller Bowman, the author of a Wyoming County history book, served as a secretary to Judge R. D. Bailey for 30 years. She also handled the judge's financial accounts and was a sister of photographer Robert R. Keller. Mary was noted for her excellent needlepoint. (Photograph courtesy of Mike Goode.)

A favorite subject of Robert R. Keller's photographs was romantic young couples. Shown at left is a couple in a swing, which was a popular place for courting couples. The photograph below shows a couple sitting on the grass. None of the individuals is identified, so it is not known whether they eventually married. In any event, they seemed to enjoy each other's company at the time. (Photographs courtesy of the Robert R. Keller collection.)

In the early years, circuit riding preachers served Pineville Methodists. In 1875, services were held in an old log school building. In 1880, the congregation erected a one-room frame church. In 1907, the Methodists laid the cornerstone to a new building, but, because of financial difficulties, workmen did not complete the Pineville Methodist Church until 1915. For a number of years, the congregation met in the temporary courthouse. The bell that now rests on the courthouse lawn was, for a time, situated in the church's belfry. The church dismantled this building in 1947 and started work on a new building, which was completed the following year. (Photograph from the Robert R. Keller collection.)

This striking building was the Center District High School (Pineville). It opened in 1909 and had four classrooms on the first floor and a large auditorium on the second floor. The structure served both grade- and high-school students until 1930. Construction workers built a brick high school in 1930. (Photograph from the Robert R. Keller collection.)

In the early 20th century, a favorite summer Sunday afternoon activity was picnicking on the banks of the Guyandotte River. After the meal, the group would enjoy climbing on logs in the river. The above photograph shows a group of 12 people. The third person from the right is Kate Keller. The picture below shows a more adventurous group on the logs some distance from the shore. Looking at the people, one gains a perspective of how massive the logs were. On the right are the wooden rails for a logging railroad. (Photographs from the Robert R. Keller collection.)

Oliver Canterbury (1881–1915), who was raised in Crany, operated this barber shop on the main street in Pineville. He also sold ice cream, which made him very popular with the children. The photograph at right (c. 1910) shows him with a prize pike he caught in the Guyandotte River on his traditional Monday day off from his shop. (Photographs from the Robert R. Keller collection.)

In the late 19th century and early 20th century, ladies of fashion usually wore hats in public. The photograph shows these well-dressed ladies on a boardwalk in Pineville around 1914. The lady in the middle is Nellie Ruth Hoover Keller, and the lady on the far right is Mary Keller Bowman. (Photographs from the Robert R. Keller collection.)

Animals were another favorite subject of photographer Robert R. Keller. In this picture, he placed a hat on a donkey's head to produce a comic effect. The gentleman with his hand on the donkey is Joe Drumheller, who was a cashier at a Pineville bank. Apparently Mr. Drumheller got along well with animals as well as young ladies. A newspaper article reported that a number of young single women were pleased when he returned to Pineville after assisting his brother for two weeks at a bank in Thurmond (Fayette County). (Photograph from the Robert R. Keller collection.)

Walter Lusk, pictured here in this c. 1910 photograph, ran a boarding house and a general store in Pineville. "Drummers" would sell products to the general stores. They would carry their products in large trunks. They usually made their rounds of general stores twice a year—in the fall and spring. Around 1905, a pair of high leather boots would sell for $2.50 to $3. For a nickel, children could purchase a small bag of roasted peanuts (sometimes stale) with a prize. (Photograph from the Robert R. Keller collection.)

When J. J. Swope left Oceana and moved the *Wyoming Mountaineer* newspaper and his residence to Pineville in 1905, he used this building as his newspaper office. The office and printing press were located on the ground floor. Apartments occupied the second floor. (Photograph from the Robert R. Keller collection.)

In the early 20th century, photographers often took pictures of people with solemn and sober expressions on their faces. In this image, Robert R. Keller displayed his skill as a photographer, because he was able to show people with more relaxed, natural poses. This image (*c.* 1910) shows leaders of the Pineville community. They are, from left to right, Charley Short, Dr. J. B. Early, and Dr. J. A. Chafin. Short was the sheriff of Wyoming County (1913–1916). Dr. Early was a dentist, and Dr. Chafin was a physician. (Photograph from the Robert R. Keller collection.)

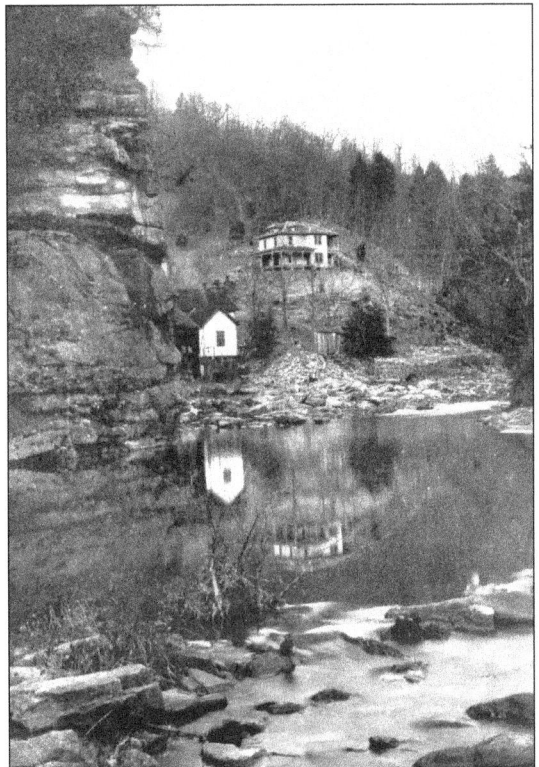

This impressive two-story house, the Judge R. D. Bailey House, is one of the finest in Wyoming County. This *c.* 1910 photograph was taken from across the Guyandotte River. The house is now adjacent to the courthouse complex in Pineville. The large stone formation in the left of the photograph is Castle Rock. The reflection of the house in the Guyandotte River gives the photograph a most interesting quality. (Photograph from the Robert R. Keller collection.)

Chivalry was alive and well on this sunny day in Pineville in the early 20th century. The photograph at right shows a gentleman gallantly holding an umbrella, shielding a lady and her baby from the sun. The photograph below shows Nina Cook holding an umbrella for protection from the sun while talking with her sister, Laura. Laura worked c. 1914 as a telephone operator in Pineville. (Photographs from the Robert R. Keller collection.)

In the early 20th century, there was an influx of European immigrants to Wyoming County. Most of them worked in the mines, but a number of the immigrants were highly skilled stonecutters. Italian stonecutters worked on two of Wyoming County's most impressive buildings—the courthouse and the Itmann Company Store. The c. 1915 photograph below shows workmen constructing the courthouse at Pineville. (Italian stonecutter photograph from the Robert R. Keller collection; courthouse photograph courtesy of Roger Lester.)

Ten members of the Guyandotte Baptist Church established the Rockcastle Baptist Church in 1858. Rockcastle Baptist Church did not have a meeting house until after 1870. A log church was built at Rockview in 1874. A frame church was erected by church members in 1899. Since its inception, the church has been active except during the Civil War years. The renowned Rev. W. H. H. Cook served as pastor of the church for almost 50 years. The Rev. G. P. Goode, longtime Wyoming County historian, was the church's clerk for more than 40 years. (Photograph courtesy of Mike Goode.)

The Wyoming County Genealogy Society published the very informative *Wyoming County Heritage Book* in 1995. One of the major activities of the society is the cataloging of the county's cemeteries. The photograph shows the officers. Pictured from left to right, they are David Brooks (treasurer), Pat Green Adams (president), Betty Bower Webber (vice president), and Juanita Adams Barnett (secretary). (Photograph courtesy of Juanita Adams Barnett.)

David Morgan first settled in the area later to be known as Baileysville about 1804. James Bailey bought the Morgan farm in 1814. Eventually Bailey developed a prosperous plantation, and the town of Baileysville grew to become a thriving community. Pictured above is the Baileysville bridge under construction over the Guyandotte River in the early 20th century. (Photograph from the Robert R. Keller Collection.)

This c. 1910 photograph shows Otis "Oat" Bailey on the left preparing to carry mail from the Baileysville Post Office to the town of Davy in McDowell County. With the impending creation of the R. D. Bailey Dam, the post office department closed the post office in 1974. The Baileysville Post Office, established in 1873, had served the community for more than 100 years. (Photograph courtesy of Roger Lester.)

Theodore Bailey (1839–1926) built this 16-room hotel in Baileysville in 1908. This photograph, taken about 1916, shows, from left to right, Bess Bailey, Lee Bailey, Martha Bailey, Troy Stone, Ruby Cook (Layman), Theodore Bailey, and Maude Stone. Lee was Theodore's son, and Martha was Theodore's wife. Theodore was a Confederate soldier who fought in a number of battles. Bailey was an industrious and enterprising individual. At various times, he was a teacher, farmer, merchant, deputy sheriff, hotel owner, lumberman, and postmaster. (Photograph courtesy of William Bailey.)

Theodore Bailey established this store in Baileysville in 1870. It stayed open until the 1940s. This *c.* 1912 photograph shows the men's department when Theodore's son, Lee, operated the store. (Photograph from the Robert R. Keller collection.)

This interesting photograph, taken c. 1910, shows the interior of an old one-room log school in Center District with a wood stove, blackboard, a picture of Abraham Lincoln, an apple on the desk, and a recitation bench. In the 19th and early 20th centuries, students were required to come to the front of the room, sit on the recitation bench, and recite their lessons. (Photograph from the Robert R. Keller collection.)

This photograph, taken in the early 1950s, shows a class at the Baileysville Grade School. Pictured in rows that run from front to back are the following (first row) Morris Davis, Mary Lou Meadows, James Hill, Robert Dalton, unidentified, Kenneth Johnston, and Alvin Kennedy; (second row) Helen Short, Patsy Short, Shirley Morgan, Ronnie Morgan, Carol Walls, Nancy McLaughlin, and Madeline Bishop; (third row) Mike Shannon, Sally Short, Mary Lou Miller, Bobby Stafford, and unidentified; (fourth row, next to windows) Gary Toler, Stanley Toler, Eleanor Tilley, unidentified, Kate West, and Bob Harmon (teacher). This school was in operation until 1974, when workmen constructed the new Baileysville Elementary and Junior High School. (Photograph courtesy of Linda Morgan Toler.)

In the early 1970s, the federal government condemned most of the land in the Baileysville area due to the impending construction of the R. D. Bailey Dam and the eventual high waters. Most of the residents moved away. Virgil Morgan and his wife, Bessie, stayed. The disbanding of the church he had attended for more than 50 years, the Baileysville Methodist Church, which was established in 1849, was especially disheartening to Morgan. To keep the spirit of Baileysville alive, he erected this 10-by-12-foot chapel on a steep hill close to his home. Morgan installed brown paneling on the walls and a red carpet on the floor in the interior of the church. This photograph shows Virgil and Bessie walking up the hill to the church. The stones next to the church are from the Bailey Hotel. Every Sunday for 15 years, he climbed the hill, rang the church bell, and prayed. Even waist-deep snow did not deter him from this routine of dedication. In 1991, he got very ill and was no longer able to visit his chapel. The bell no longer tolls. (Photograph courtesy of Leo Chabot and the *Charleston Gazette*, with thanks to Linda Morgan Toler.)

The Brenton area was first settled in 1800 by James Shannon, son-in-law of Edward McDonald. Among the earlier settlers of Brenton were this couple, Andrew Miller and his wife, Susan Adams Miller. Miller, a farmer, came to the area c. 1825. The community, first known as Bartley, was named for a local landowner, Bartley Rose. Since there was another town named Bartley in West Virginia, the post office department requested a name change, and Brenton was selected. (Photograph courtesy of Dorothy Miller Green.)

Despite this visual evidence, Wyoming County really did not have any cowboys. Oakie Miller (1906–1987) selected this outfit from the costumes that a traveling photographer had in stock. Oakie was a coal miner at Marianna. (Photograph courtesy of Dorothy Miller Green.)

This house was the old Ellis homestead in Hanover. The Ellis family members were prominent early residents in the area. The first postmaster of Hanover was A. E. Ellis. In 1891, he proposed that the post office be named for him—it was not an uncommon practice in those days for the post office to be named for the prospective postmaster—but the post office department rejected that name, and Hanover was chosen. (Photograph courtesy of Mike Goode.)

This early-20th-century photograph shows Poeten Davis on the left and Aubrey Davis standing next to the Hanover Post Office and in front of the Maggie Weeks house. The post office department named Poeten Davis postmaster in 1905. Hanover is the largest community in Huff Creek District. In 1908, in addition to the post office, the town had a Baptist church, two general stores, two blacksmiths, a photographer, a gristmill, a constable, and a justice of the peace. (Photograph courtesy of Roger Lester.)

In the late 19th and early 20th century, churches often used schools for their services and programs. This c. 1910 photograph shows the Trace Fork School of North Spring when it was being used for a church service. A horse is pictured on the left. The existing roads often needed improvements, and the principal modes of transportation were walking or riding a horse. (Photograph courtesy of Roger Lester.)

The North Spring Post Office is one of the oldest in the county. The post office department established it in 1875. The post office derived its name from the fact that there was a large spring near the farm of Armour Godfrey called "the Old North Spring." Godrey was its first postmaster and served in that position for 26 years. Shown here is a photograph of the current post office. (Photograph by the author.)

Eight

MULLENS AND VICINITY

The fire of 1919 that ravaged the central business district of Mullens destroyed this original Virginian train station. The cow on the left of this c. 1914 photograph underscores the fact that the community was still in a transitional phase between a rural town and an industrial one. (Photograph from the Robert R. Keller collection.)

This c. 1915 photograph shows a view of the town of Mullens. In the extreme lower left corner is the railroad station. Directly across the street is the Busy Bee Restaurant. Next to the restaurant is the Railroad and Miners Pharmacy. Next is the George W. Graham general store. Behind the Graham Store was a grocery store owned by A. J. Mullins, the town's founder. Across the street on the corner is the Bank of Mullens building. The three-story white building behind the bank is the Ben Dunham Hotel. (Photograph courtesy of Twin Falls State Park.)

A. J. Mullins (1857–1938), who founded the town of Mullens in 1894, was a dynamic, hard-working individual who engaged in a number of diverse activities. At various times, Mullins ran a store and served as postmaster (1905–1909), a justice of peace and a preacher, and operated a sawmill. (Mullens was named for him, but on some legal documents the "i" was not dotted, and the town has been known as "Mullens" ever since.) A. J. Mullins was elected the town's first mayor and served in the state legislature (1915–1917). (Photograph courtesy of the West Virginia State Archives.)

D. D. Moran, like A. J. Mullins, was an early leader of Mullens. There were several common aspects to their backgrounds. They both served as postmasters, mayors, bank presidents, and delegates in the state legislature. Moran also was a brilliant attorney and was Wyoming County's prosecuting attorney from 1929 to 1932. Moran Avenue, one of the principal streets in Mullens, is named for D. D. Moran. (Photograph courtesy of the West Virginia State Archives.)

The first Bank of Mullens building, a two-story edifice located on the corner of First Street and Moran Avenue, was destroyed in the fire of 1919. Workers rebuilt this building on the original site the following year. The new building was a three-story structure with the bank on the first floor and other offices on the second and third levels. (Photograph courtesy of Susan Robinson.)

The prospect of coal mining and railroad jobs attracted immigrants from Europe to Wyoming County in the early 20th century. The photograph to the left shows Luigi and Speranza Camerese with their grandson, Joe. They settled in Mullens. Joe was killed during World War II. The picture below shows the Camereses' daughter, Flora (1893–1929), with her husband, Andrew D'Antoni (1886–1976). For a few years, Andrew worked in the coal mines, and then he established a grocery store in Mullens. (Photographs courtesy of Lewis D'Antoni.)

The Mead Poca Building (photograph damaged in 2001 flood) first served as the headquarters for John C. Sullivan's extensive mining interest. Sullivan was part owner of the Wyoming Hotel, and he helped establish the Mullens newspaper and the first Catholic church in the county. Dr. Ward Wilie opened the Wylie Hospital in the building in 1937. The picture below shows some of the hospital staff. They are, from left to right, Elsie Tolliver, unidentified, Dr. Wylie, two unidentified people, and Maxine Davis. (Photographs courtesy of Jack Feller and Betty Wylie Farmer.)

One of the most imposing churches in Wyoming County is the Highland Avenue Baptist Church in Mullens. Jubal Early, who constructed many buildings in the Mullens area, built the church in 1923. This striking three-story structure overlooks the central business district of the town, and the church is designed in the shape of a cross. An eloquent cupola graces the center of the cross-shaped roof. (Photograph courtesy of Frances McGhee Bright.)

Rev. J. M. Criswell is shown here with the choir of the Highland Avenue Baptist Church. The lady at the far end of the second row from the right is Frances McGhee Bright, a church member for 70 years. Reverend Criswell served as the minister of the church for more than 20 years. He helped design the church. When Reverend Criswell came to the church in the early 1920s, its membership was 20. In the 1940s, the congregation exceeded 400. The Mullens community mourned the passing of the beloved minister in 1945. (Photograph courtesy of Frances McGhee Bright.)

The Mullens Women Club engaged in numerous civic activities. A prime project of the club was the improvement of the community's parks and playgrounds. In 1956 and 1957, the club won first prize in the state small club division for outstanding community work. The *Readers Digest* magazine in 1962 honored the club with a national award for a street lighting project. This 1953 photograph shows the following club members from left to right: (first row) Mrs. Dollie Harmon, Mrs. N. D. Trent, Josephine Snyder, Mrs. Carl Price, Janis Roten, Mrs. Dan Shuman, Mrs. Elbert Cook, Elizabeth Cook, unidentified, and Mrs. C. V. Feller; (second row) Mrs. Walter McConehey, Mrs. Troy Stone, unidentified, Helen Hall, unidentified, Harriet Hall, unidentified, Helen Smith, Mrs. Sam White, and Mae Belcher; (third row) unidentified, Mary Campbell, Mrs. R. L. Hart, Mrs. Josephine Williams, Mrs. Gilbert Cook, Mrs. Lacitisha Morgan, Mrs. Martha Stone, Effie Delp, Josephine Danwood, Kathleen Carr, Elizabeth Duncan, Mrs. J. B. Swope, and Mrs. Paul Vires. (Photograph courtesy of Twin Falls State Park; thanks to Elizabeth Duncan for the identifications.)

With help from other Mullens residents, William "Sarge" McGhee has painted a number of murals. Some murals are inside buildings, while others are on the exterior walls. They are not only very attractive but help to graphically preserve the rich history of the town. The 35-by-56-foot mural above depicts the homecoming of World War I veterans in 1918. The 20-by-90-foot mural below shows Virginian Railway Engine No. 215 pulling baggage car No. 53 and passenger cars. (Postcards courtesy of Jack Feller.)

Jack Feller is shown here standing by the Mullens Caboose Museum. Tragically, the 2001 flood destroyed hundreds of historic photographs housed in the museum. Feller has authored five books chronicling the history of Mullens from 1894 to 1946 and has been involved in a host of civic activities. Scott Durham paid him a high compliment. He said, "If there is anything positive happening in Wyoming County, there is a good chance Jack has had a hand in it." Feller was one of the individuals who spearheaded the creation of Twin Falls State Park. (Photograph by the author.)

Beautiful Twin Falls State Park opened in 1970. The park is located in a scenic, mountainous area with an elevation close to 2,500 feet. Visitors have opportunities to enjoy a wide range of activities including camping, golfing, hiking, picnicking, swimming, and nature programs. In addition, the park offers a diverse calendar of programs, including the Bear Hole 10K Road Race, photography workshops, and the Lumberjackin' Bluegrassin' Jamboree. Accommodations at the popular lodge are being expanded. (Photograph courtesy of Twin Falls State Park.)

The Bower homestead (Pioneer Farm) is now part of Twin Falls State Park. Hamilton and Virginia Bower moved into the c. 1835 home in 1866. The house is probably the oldest remaining building in the county. In 1895, their son, Wiley Bower (1867–1959) and his wife, Teenie, set up housekeeping in the home. In 1915, the home was expanded when Wiley built a seven-room frame house around the cabin. After the land became part of the state park in 1965, workers were razing the building and discovered the original structure, which was then preserved. (Photograph courtesy of Susan Robinson.)

Wiley Bower stands with his children, Charlie and Susie, in this photograph taken around 1908. The bull is named Curly. The Bower farm produced a wide variety of crops. Teenie Bower endeavored to keep the basement of the house stocked with 1,000 canned meats, fruits, and vegetables. In 1928, a church association held a meeting nearby. At their invitation, the Bowers served 250 people a meal. Seventy-five people spent the night. There were people sleeping in the hayloft, on the cabin floor, on the porch, and in the yard. (Photograph courtesy of Twin Falls State Park.)

The Bower School is located in the present confines of Twin Falls State Park. This photograph shows the students of the school around 1910. Pictured from left to right are (first row) Floyd Houck, John Houck, Wade Houck, Maltida Bower, three unidentified children, Charles Bower, Lucy Bower, unidentified, Viola Adkins, Rose Adkins, and unidentified; (second row) Winfred Houck, Oliver Adkins, Jeanette Bower, two unidentified children, Mary Meadows (teacher), unidentified, Blanche Houck, Mary Houck, Bill Adkins, Mose Adkins, and Fitchue Houck. (Photograph courtesy of Betty Bower Blankenship.)

Architect Alex B. Mahood (1881–1970) designed a number of buildings on the National Register of Historic Places, including the Itmann Company Store and Office. He built it for the coal company serving Itmann. Mahood studied at the Ecole Des Beaux-Arts in Paris, France. In Wyoming County, in addition to the Itmann Company Store, he designed the Wyoming Hotel in Mullens and Glen Rogers's second community center building. (Photograph courtesy of ERCA.)

I. T. Mann (1863–1932) was the president of the Bramwell, Mercer County (West Virginia) bank, which once was regarded as the richest little bank in America. At one time, Mann controlled nine profitable banks, and his financial holdings included real estate, lumber, and coal mines. In 1916, his coal company opened a mine in Wyoming County. The coal camp was named Itmann based on his name. Prior to the Great Depression, Mann had amassed a fortune valued over $80 million, but he lost most of it in the financial crisis that gripped the nation. (Photograph courtesy of ERCA.)

One of the most impressive public buildings in West Virginia is the Itmann Company Store. The building, completed in 1920, is made of local, rough-faced sandstone and is on the National Register of Historic Places. A number of European immigrants, particularly Italian stone masons, worked on the building. The building reflects elements of the Classical Revival style. The company store was the center of the community. (Photograph courtesy of ERCA.)

This photograph of Susie Tolliver Phillips of Saulsville was taken in 1917. She attended Concord College and was an elementary school teacher on Bower Ridge. In 1921, she married Lacy Phillips, and they had eight children, including seven sons. Lacy was a farmer, and he had 20 dairy cattle. The cattle feed came in sacks with a flower pattern. Susie made bed linens, dresses, curtains, and dish towels from the empty feed sacks, displaying a resourcefulness that was characteristic of many women of her generation. (Photograph courtesy of Shirley Blankenship Phillips.)

Quilt-making has been a Wyoming County tradition for many years. Shirley Blankenship Phillips proudly displays a beautiful quilt with a pattern of migrating geese she made. She has been making quilts for 50 years. Frequently such quilts stay in a family for generations, with successive mothers passing the quilt on to their daughters. (Photograph courtesy of Shirley Blankenship Phillips.)

The Wyco Coal Mine and town were created by the Wyoming Coal Company in 1914. The Wyco mines were very productive and operated for many years. Wyco once was considered the prettiest coal camp in the area. There were annual contests to determine who had the town's most attractive garden and lawn. The photograph above shows the superintendent's house in the background and the recreation hall in the foreground. The recreation hall, which was torn down years ago, once housed a theatre, restaurant, and pool hall. Pictured below is Wyco's company store. (Photograph courtesy of Sante Boninsegna.)

Three of the most prominent houses in Wyco were the houses shown above. The company store manager lived in the house on the left, the company doctor resided in the middle house, while the mine foreman lived in the house on the right. Dr. George Fordham was the company doctor at Wyco for 30 years, and he lived in the house in the center. The photograph below shows Dr. Fordham's identification card when he served as a doctor in World War I. (Photographs courtesy of Sante Boninsegna and George Fordham Jr.)

This building once housed the Miller Pocahontas Coal Company Store in Corinne. In 1921, the coal company was instrumental in getting the community of Corinne incorporated. The coal company shut down in 1930, and the community ceased providing municipal services. The court recalled its charter in 1932. The post office was once located in this building. Pictured is Margaret J. Lafferty Lusk, who served as postmaster for more than 20 years. (Photograph courtesy of Margaret J. Lafferty Lusk.)

Carl Scholz, a German born in 1872, came to the United States around 1890 and soon made a strong reputation for skill in mining operations. An associate of H. H. Rogers asked Scholz to start mining operations in Wyoming County. By mid-1922, the mine was in operation. Glen Rogers soon became the most productive mine served by the Virginian Railway. In fewer than four decades, it produced 24 million tons of coal. This production came, however, at a high price. At Glen Rogers, 160 miners lost their lives. (Photograph courtesy of Karl Lilly III and Bud Perry.)

J. W. Marland (1894–1972) became the mine superintendent at Glen Rogers in 1926, and his skillful management was a major factor in Glen Rogers becoming one of the leading mines in the county and the state. He was a hard taskmaster with a fiery temperament. Nevertheless he related well with his diverse ethnic work crew, who regarded him as tough but fair. He told his workers, "Never tell me a lie. If you tell me the truth, I'll stick by you. If you tell me a lie, you're in trouble." (Photograph courtesy of Karl Lilly III and Bud Perry.)

This picture shows the town center of Glen Rogers, which was dominated by the 289-foot smokestack. When the town of Glen Rogers was formed, it was very isolated. Construction crews built roads and railroad tracks to the community. Carl Scholz named the town. Glen is a Scottish word meaning narrow, secluded valley, and Rogers was in honor of H. H. Rogers. (Photograph courtesy of Karl Lilly III and Bud Perry.)

Many of Glen Rogers's commercial buildings and some of the houses were made of brick. The four-story Glen Rogers Hotel, shown here, was one of the brick buildings. The hotel dining room, noted for its good food, was a favorite place of J. W. Marland, the long-time mine superintendent. Marland insisted that the dining room keep an ample supply of fruit pies and cobblers on hand. (Photograph courtesy of ERCA.)

These brick duplex houses in Glen Rogers were very unusual for a coal town. Most coal camp houses were of frame construction, and Glen Rogers had some of these as well. Workmen built these houses from bricks made at Glen Rogers's brick plant. (Photograph courtesy of the ERCA.)

Most coalfield houses of worship were nondenominational community churches as was the case with this Glen Rogers church. The Glen Rogers church was well-attended and a source of pride for the town. Donzella Nuckols, the mother of famed basketball coach Don Nuckols, was the church pianist for many years. She was also a local correspondent for the *Beckley Herald* newspaper of Raleigh County, West Virginia. (Church photograph courtesy of Karl Lilly III and Bud Perry; Donzella Nuckols photograph courtesy of Don Nuckols.)

Pictured here is a scene of Herndon around 1910. The post office department established an office here in 1898. When the federal authorities rejected the proposed name of Otter, the post office was named in honor of Herndon M. Cline, a local resident. In the early 20th century, Herndon was a logging town, and later it was also a coal mining town. On the lumber end, there was a company store, doctor's office, and a large boarding house. On the mining end, there was the railroad station, theatre, and large community church. (Photograph courtesy of Marie McKinney Pedneau.)

This 1935 photograph shows the Herndon Methodist Church Sunday school class. People identified on the third row from the front are Venni Fitzwater (first person from left), Olive Reece (third person from left), Beulah McKinney (dark blouse), and Marie McKinney (ninth person from left). In the fourth row, Raymond McKinney is the third boy from the left. He was killed during World War II in France. People identified on the back row are Edna McKinney (first person from left), Cora Glover (third person from left, an elementary school teacher), Vida McKinney (black hat) and George Fitzwater (last person from left, the Sunday school superintendent). (Photograph courtesy of Marie McKinney Pedneau.)

Around 1915, John C. Sullivan established two coal mines at Tralee: the Barkers Creek Coal Company and the Harty Coal Company. He named the coal town Tralee in honor of his mother's home in Ireland. Barkers Creek's most productive year was 1923, when 86,980 tons of coal were mined, while Harty's best year was 1925, when 109,082 tons were produced. This 1923 photograph shows the coal camp of Tralee. Very little of the former town remains. (Photograph courtesy of Edgar Goad.)

The first McKinney settled at Basin in 1845. The McKinney family reunion was one of the largest in the county, attracting 2,000 people in the 1930s. This 1917 photograph shows Big Jim McKinney's family at Basin. Pictured from left to right are the following: (first row) Big Jim McKinney and two unidentified relatives; (second row) Arthur McKinney, unidentified, George McKinney, unidentified, Jasper McKinney, and Martha McKinney. Arthur, George, Jasper, and Martha were children of Big Jim. George served as constable of the Barkers Ridge District for 20 years. Big Jim was a postmaster at Basin. (Photograph courtesy of Marie McKinney Pedneau.)

The post office department established a post office at Devils Fork in 1915. In the mid-1930s, the name of the community was changed to Stephenson. This 1940s photograph shows the Buckeye Coal Company Store at Stephenson. Next to the store is the superintendent's house. The two-story building behind the superintendent's house is a boarding house. One of the most productive years for the Buckeye mine was 1943, when 278,460 tons of coal were mined. (Photograph courtesy of Janet Blankenship Meadows.)

Evelyn Belcher is shown here with her sons, Jesse (foreground) and Pete (background), at their home in Stephenson. The boys had a major disappointment the year after this picture was made (1962). Their parents had purchased them bicycles for Christmas at the Buckeye Company Store. They had left them there to pick up prior to Christmas. Unfortunately, before they could pick them up, the store burned down. The boys had to wait to the next year for their bikes. When Jesse and Pete grew up, they became coal miners at the Buckeye mine. (Photograph courtesy of Pete Belcher.)

www.ingramcontent.com/pod-product-compliance
Lightning Source LLC
Chambersburg PA
CBHW050613110426
42813CB00008B/2546